Getting Started with NoSQL

Your guide to the world and technology of NoSQL

Gaurav Vaish

PUBLISHING

BIRMINGHAM - MUMBAI

Getting Started with NoSQL

First published: March 2013

Production Reference: 1150313

Published by Packt Publishing Ltd.
Livery Place
35 Livery Street
Birmingham B3 2PB, UK.

ISBN 978-1-84969-4-988

www.packtpub.com

Cover Image by Will Kewley (william.kewley@kbbs.ie)

Credits

Author
Gaurav Vaish

Reviewer
Satish Kowkuntla

Acquisition Editor
Robin de Jonh

Commissioning Editor
Maria D'souza

Technical Editors
Worrell Lewis
Varun Pius Rodrigues

Project Coordinator
Amigya Khurana

Proofreader
Elinor Perry-Smith

Indexer
Rekha Nair

Graphics
Aditi Gajjar

Production Coordinator
Pooja Chiplunkar

Cover Work
Pooja Chiplunkar

About the Author

Gaurav Vaish works as Principal Engineer with Yahoo! India. He works primarily in three domains—cloud, web, and devices including mobile, connected TV, and the like. His expertise lies in designing and architecting applications for the same.

Gaurav started his career in 2002 with Adobe Systems India working in their engineering solutions group.

In 2005, he started his own company Edujini Labs focusing on corporate training and collaborative learning.

He holds a B. Tech. in Electrical Engineering with specialization in Speech Signal Processing from IIT Kanpur.

He runs his personal blog at www.mastergaurav.com and www.m10v.com.

This book would not have been complete without support from my wife, Renu, who was a big inspiration in writing. She ensured that after a day's hard work at the office when I sat down to write the book, I was all charged up. At times, when I wanted to take a break off, she pushed me to completion by keeping a tab on the schedule. And she ensured me great food or a cup of tea whenever I needed it.

This book would not have the details that I have been able to provide had it not been timely and useful inputs from Satish Kowkuntla, Architect at Yahoo! He ensured that no relevant piece of information was missed out. He gave valuable insights to writing the correct language keeping the reader in mind. Had it not been for him, you may not have seen the book in the shape that it is in.

About the Reviewer

Satish Kowkuntla is a software engineer by profession with over 20 years of experience in software development, design, and architecture. Satish is currently working as a software architect at Yahoo! and his experience is in the areas of web technologies, frontend technologies, and digital home technologies. Prior to Yahoo! Satish has worked in several companies in the areas of digital home technologies, system software, CRM software, and engineering CAD software. Much of his career has been in Silicon Valley.

www.PacktPub.com

Support files, eBooks, discount offers and more

You might want to visit www.PacktPub.com for support files and downloads related to your book.

Did you know that Packt offers eBook versions of every book published, with PDF and ePub files available? You can upgrade to the eBook version at www.PacktPub.com and as a print book customer, you are entitled to a discount on the eBook copy. Get in touch with us at service@packtpub.com for more details.

At www.PacktPub.com, you can also read a collection of free technical articles, sign up for a range of free newsletters and receive exclusive discounts and offers on Packt books and eBooks.

http://PacktLib.PacktPub.com

Do you need instant solutions to your IT questions? PacktLib is Packt's online digital book library. Here, you can access, read and search across Packt's entire library of books.

Why Subscribe?

* Fully searchable across every book published by Packt
* Copy and paste, print and bookmark content
* On demand and accessible via web browser

Free Access for Packt account holders

If you have an account with Packt at www.PacktPub.com, you can use this to access PacktLib today and view nine entirely free books. Simply use your login credentials for immediate access.

Dedicated to Renu Chandel, my wife.

Table of Contents

Preface

This book takes a deep dive in NoSQL as technology providing a comparative study on the data models, the products in the market, and with RDBMS using scenario-driven case studies

Relational databases have been used to store data for decades while SQL has been the de-facto language to interact with RDBMS. In the last few years, NoSQL has been a growing choice especially for large, web-scale applications. Non-relational databases provide the scale and speed that you may need for your application.

However, making a decision to start with or switch to NoSQL requires more insights than a few benchmarks—knowing the options at hand, advantages and drawbacks, scenarios where it suits the most, and where it should be avoided are very critical to making a decision.

This book is a from-the-ground-up guide that takes you from the very definition to a real-world application. It provides you step-by-step approach to design and implement a NoSQL application that will help you make clear decisions on database choice, database model choice, and the related parameters. The book is suited for a developer, an architect, as well as a CTO.

What this book covers

Chapter 1, Overview and Architecture, gives you a head-start into NoSQL. It helps you understand what NoSQL is and is not, and also provides you with insights into the question – "Why NoSQL?"

Chapter 2, Characteristics of NoSQL, takes a dig into the RDBMS problems that NoSQL attempts to solve and substantiates it with a concrete scenario.

Chapter 3, NoSQL Storage Types, explores various storage types available in the market today with a deep dive – comparing and contrasting them, and identifying what to use when.

Chapter 4, Advantages and Drawbacks, brings out the advantages and drawbacks of using NoSQL by taking a scenario-based approach to understand the possibilities and limitations.

Chapter 5, Comparative Study of NoSQL Products, does a detailed comparative study of ten NoSQL databases on about 25 parameters, both technical and non-technical.

Chapter 6, Case Study, takes you through a simple application implemented using NoSQL. It covers various scenarios possible in the application and approaches that can be used with NoSQL database.

Appendix, Taxonomy, introduces you to the common and not-so-common terms that we come across while dealing with NoSQL. It will also enable you to read through and understand the literature available on the Internet or otherwise.

What you need for this book

To run the examples in the book the following software will be required:

- Operating System—Ubuntu or any other Linux variant is preferred
- CouchDB will be required to take a dig into document store in *Chapter 3, NoSQL Storage Types*
- Java SDK, Eclipse, Google App Engine SDK, and Objectify will be required to cover the examples of column-oriented databases in *Chapter 3, NoSQL Storage Types*
- Redis will be required to cover the examples of key-value store in *Chapter 3, NoSQL Storage Types*
- Neo4J will be required to cover the examples of graph store in *Chapter 3, NoSQL Storage Types*
- MongoDB to run through the case study covered in *Chapter 3, NoSQL Storage Types*

The latest versions are preferable.

Who this book is for

This book is a great resource for someone starting with NoSQL and indispensable literature for technology decision makers — be it architect, product manager or CTO.

It is assumed that you have a background in RDBMS modeling and SQL and have had exposure to at least one of the programming languages — Java or JavaScript.

It is also assumed that you have at least heard about NoSQL and are interested to explore the same but nothing beyond that. You are not expected to know the meaning and purpose of NoSQL — this book provides all inputs from the groundup.

Whether you are a developer or an architect or a CTO of a company, this book is an indispensable resource for you to have in your library.

Conventions

In this book, you will find a number of styles of text that distinguish between different kinds of information. Here are some examples of these styles, and an explanation of their meaning.

Code words in text, database table names, folder names, filenames, file extensions, pathnames, dummy URLs, user input, and Twitter handles are shown as follows: "Do you remember the JOIN query that you wrote to collate the data across multiple tables to create your final view?"

A block of code is set as follows:

```
"_id": "98ef65e7-52e4-4466-bacc-3a8dc0c15c79",
"firstName": "Gaurav",
"lastName": "Vaish",
"department": "f0adcbf5-7389-4491-9c42-f39a9d3d4c75",
"homeAddress": {
    "_id": "fa62fd39-17f8-4a16-80d6-71a5b71d758d",
    "line1": "123, 45th Main"
    "city" : "NoSQLLand",
    "country": "India",
    "zipCode": "123456"
}
```

When we wish to draw your attention to a particular part of a code block, the relevant lines or items are set in bold:

```
"_id": "98ef65e7-52e4-4466-bacc-3a8dc0c15c79",
"firstName": "Gaurav",
"lastName": "Vaish",
```

```
"department": "f0adcbf5-7389-4491-9c42-f39a9d3d4c75",
"homeAddress": {
    "_id": "fa62fd39-17f8-4a16-80d6-71a5b71d758d",
    "line1": "123, 45th Main"
    "city" : "NoSQLLand",
    "country": "India",
    "zipCode": "123456"
}
```

Any command-line input or output is written as follows:

```
curl -X PUT -H "Content-Type: application/json" \
```

New terms and **important words** are shown in bold. Words that you see on the screen, in menus or dialog boxes for example, appear in the text like this: "clicking the **Next** button moves you to the next screen".

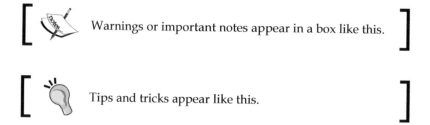

> Warnings or important notes appear in a box like this.

> Tips and tricks appear like this.

Reader feedback

Feedback from our readers is always welcome. Let us know what you think about this book—what you liked or may have disliked. Reader feedback is important for us to develop titles that you really get the most out of.

To send us general feedback, simply send an e-mail to feedback@packtpub.com, and mention the book title via the subject of your message.

If there is a topic that you have expertise in and you are interested in either writing or contributing to a book, see our author guide on www.packtpub.com/authors.

Customer support

Now that you are the proud owner of a Packt book, we have a number of things to help you to get the most from your purchase.

Downloading the color images of this book

We also provide you a PDF file that has color images of the screenshots/diagrams used in this book. The color images will help you better understand the changes in the output. You can download this file from `http://www.packtpub.com/sites/default/files/downloads/5689_graphics.pdf`.

Errata

Although we have taken every care to ensure the accuracy of our content, mistakes do happen. If you find a mistake in one of our books—maybe a mistake in the text or the code—we would be grateful if you would report this to us. By doing so, you can save other readers from frustration and help us improve subsequent versions of this book. If you find any errata, please report them by visiting `http://www.packtpub.com/submit-errata`, selecting your book, clicking on the **errata submission form** link, and entering the details of your errata. Once your errata are verified, your submission will be accepted and the errata will be uploaded on our website, or added to any list of existing errata, under the Errata section of that title. Any existing errata can be viewed by selecting your title from `http://www.packtpub.com/support`.

Piracy

Piracy of copyright material on the Internet is an ongoing problem across all media. At Packt, we take the protection of our copyright and licenses very seriously. If you come across any illegal copies of our works, in any form, on the Internet, please provide us with the location address or website name immediately so that we can pursue a remedy.

Please contact us at `copyright@packtpub.com` with a link to the suspected pirated material.

We appreciate your help in protecting our authors, and our ability to bring you valuable content.

Questions

You can contact us at `questions@packtpub.com` if you are having a problem with any aspect of the book, and we will do our best to address it.

An Overview of NoSQL

1

Now that you have got this book in your hand, you must be both excited and anxious about NoSQL. In this chapter, we get a head-start on:

- What NoSQL is
- What NoSQL is not
- Why NoSQL
- A list of NoSQL databases

For over decades, relational databases have been used to store what we know as structured data. The data is sub-divided into groups, referred to as **tables**. The tables store well-defined units of data in terms of type, size, and other constraints. Each unit of data is known as **column** while each unit of the group is known as **row**. The columns may have relationships defined across themselves, for example parent-child, and hence the name relational databases. And because consistency is one of the critical factors, scaling horizontally is a challenging task, if not impossible.

About a decade earlier, with the rise of large web applications, research has poured into handling data at scale. One of the outputs of these researches is non-relational database, in general referred to as NoSQL database. One of the main problems that a NoSQL database solves is scale, among others.

Defining NoSQL

According to Wikipedia:

> In computing, NoSQL (mostly interpreted as "not only SQL") is a broad class of database management systems identified by its non-adherence to the widely used relational database management system model; that is, NoSQL databases are not primarily built on tables, and as a result, generally do not use SQL for data manipulation.

The NoSQL movement began in the early years of the 21st century when the world started its deep focus on creating web-scale database. By web-scale, I mean scale to cater to hundreds of millions of users and now growing to billions of connected devices including but not limited to mobiles, smartphones, internet TV, in-car devices, and many more.

Although Wikipedia treats it as "not only SQL", NoSQL originally started off as a simple combination of two words—No and SQL—clearly and completely visible in the new term. No acronym. What it literally means is, "I do not want to use SQL". To elaborate, "I want to access database without using any SQL syntax". Why? We shall explore the in a while.

Whatever be the root phrase, NoSQL today is the term used to address to the class of databases that do not follow **relational database management system (RDBMS)** principles, specifically being that of ACID nature, and are specifically designed to handle the speed and scale of the likes of Google, Facebook, Yahoo, Twitter, and many more.

History

Before we take a deep dive into it, let us set our context right by exploring some key landmarks in history that led to the birth of NoSQL.

From Inktomi, probably the first true search engine, to Google, the present world leader, the computer scientists have well recognized the limitations of the traditional and widely used RDBMS specifically related to the issues of scalability, parallelization, and cost, also noting that the data set is minimally cross-referenced as compared to the chunked, transactional data, which is mostly fed to RDBMS.

Specifically, if we just take the case of Google that gets billions of requests a month across applications that may be totally unrelated in what they do but related in how they deliver, the problem of scalability is to be solved at each layer—right from data access to final delivery. Google, therefore, had to work innovatively and gave birth to a new computing ecosystem comprising of:

- **GFS**: Distributed filesystem
- **Chubby**: Distributed coordination system
- **MapReduce**: Parallel execution system
- **Big Data**: Column oriented database

These systems were initially described in papers released from 2003 to 2006 listed as follows:

- Google File System, 2003: `http://research.google.com/archive/gfs.html`

- Chubby, 2006: `http://research.google.com/archive/chubby.html`

- MapReduce, 2004: `http://research.google.com/archive/mapreduce.html`

- Big Data, 2006: `http://research.google.com/archive/bigtable.html`

These and other papers led to a spike in increased activities, specially in open source, around large scale distributed computing and some of the most amazing products were born. Some of the initial products that came up included:

- **Lucene**: Java-based indexing and search engine (`http://lucene.apache.org`)

- **Hadoop**: For reliable, scalable, distributed computing (`http://hadoop.apache.org`)

- **Cassandra**: Scalable, multi-master database with no single point of failure (`http://cassandra.apache.org`)

- **ZooKeeper**: High performance coordination service for distributed applications (`http://zookeeper.apache.org`)

- **Pig**: High level dataflow language and execution framework for parallel computation (`http://pig.apache.org`)

What NoSQL is and what it is not

Now that we have a fair idea on how this side of the world evolved, let us examine at what NoSQL is and what it is not.

NoSQL is a generic term used to refer to any data store that does not follow the traditional RDBMS model—specifically, the data is non-relational and it does not use SQL as the query language. It is used to refer to the databases that attempt to solve the problems of scalability and availability against that of atomicity or consistency.

NoSQL is not a database. It is not even a type of database. In fact, it is a term used to *filter out* (read reject) a set of databases out of the ecosystem. There are several distinct family trees available. In *Chapter 4, Advantages and Drawbacks*, we explore various types of data models (or simply, database types) available under this umbrella.

Traditional RDBMS applications have focused on **ACID** transactions:

- **Atomicity**: Everything in a transaction succeeds lest it is rolled back.
- **Consistency**: A transaction cannot leave the database in an inconsistent state.
- **Isolation**: One transaction cannot interfere with another.
- **Durability**: A completed transaction persists, even after applications restart.

Howsoever indispensible these qualities may seem, they are quite incompatible with availability and performance on applications of web-scale. For example, if a company like Amazon were to use a system like this, imagine how slow it would be. If I proceed to buy a book and a transaction is on, it will lock a part of the database, specifically the inventory, and every other person in the world will have to wait until I complete my transaction. This just doesn't work!

Amazon may use cached data or even unlocked records resulting in inconsistency. In an extreme case, you and I may end up buying the last copy of a book in the store with one of us finally receiving an apology mail. (Well, Amazon definitely has a much better system than this).

The point I am trying to make here is, we may have to look beyond ACID to something called **BASE**, coined by Eric Brewer:

- **Basic availability**: Each request is guaranteed a response—successful or failed execution.
- **Soft state**: The state of the system may change over time, at times without any input (for eventual consistency).
- **Eventual consistency**: The database may be momentarily inconsistent but will be consistent eventually.

Eric Brewer also noted that it is impossible for a distributed computer system to provide consistency, availability and partition tolerance simultaneously. This is more commonly referred to as the CAP theorem.

Note, however, that in cases like stock exchanges or banking where transactions are critical, cached or state data will just not work. So, NoSQL is, definitely, not a solution to all the database related problems

Why NoSQL?

Looking at what we have explored so far, does it mean that we should look at NoSQL only when we start reaching the problems of scale? No.

NoSQL databases have a lot more to offer than just solving the problems of scale which are mentioned as follows:

- **Schemaless data representation**: Almost all NoSQL implementations offer schemaless data representation. This means that you don't have to think too far ahead to define a structure and you can continue to evolve over time—including adding new fields or even nesting the data, for example, in case of JSON representation.

- **Development time**: I have heard stories about reduced development time because one doesn't have to deal with complex SQL queries. Do you remember the JOIN query that you wrote to collate the data across multiple tables to create your final view?

- **Speed**: Even with the small amount of data that you have, if you can deliver in milliseconds rather than hundreds of milliseconds—especially over mobile and other intermittently connected devices—you have much higher probability of winning users over.

- **Plan ahead for scalability**: You read it right. Why fall into the ditch and then try to get out of it? Why not just plan ahead so that you never fall into one. Or in other words, your application can be quite elastic—it can handle sudden spikes of load. Of course, you win users over straightaway.

List of NoSQL Databases

The buzz around NoSQL still hasn't reached its peak, at least to date. We see more offerings in the market over time. The following table is a list of some of the more mature, popular, and powerful NoSQL databases segregated by data model used:

Document	Key-Value	XML	Column	Graph
MongoDB	Redis	BaseX	BigTable	Neo4J
CouchDB	Membase	eXist	Hadoop / HBase	FlockDB
RavenDB	Voldemort		Cassandra	InfiniteGraph
Terrastore	MemcacheDB		SimpleDB	
			Cloudera	

This list is by no means comprehensive, nor does it claim to be. One of the positive points about this list is that most of the databases in the list are open source and community driven.

Chapter 4, Advantages and Drawbacks, provides an in-depth study of the various popular data models used in NoSQL databases.

Chapter 6, Case Study, does an exhaustive comparison of some of these databases along various key parameters including, but not limited to, data model, language, performance, license, price, community, resources, extensibility, and many more.

Summary

In this chapter, we learned about the fundamentals of NoSQL—what it is all about and more critically, what it is not. We took a splash in the history to appreciate the reasons and science behind it. You are recommended to explore the web for historical events around this to take a deep dive in appreciating it.

NoSQL is not a solution to each and every application. It is worth noting that most of the products do throw away the traditional ACID nature giving way to BASE infrastructure. Having said that, some products standout—CouchDB and Neo4j, for example, are ACID compliant NoSQL databases.

Adopting NoSQL is not only a technological change but also change in mindset, behaviour and thought process meaning that if you plan to hire a developer to work with NoSQL, he/she must understand the new models.

In the next chapter, we will have a quick look at the taxonomy and jack up our vocabulary before we dive deeply into NoSQL.

2
Characteristics of NoSQL

For decades, software engineers have been developing applications with relational databases in mind. The literature, architectures, frameworks, and toolkits have all been written keeping in mind the relational structure between the entities.

The famous **entity-relationship diagrams**, or more commonly known as **ER diagrams**, form the basis for database design. And for quite some time now, engineers have used **object-relational mapping (O/RM)** tools to help them model relationships — is-a, has, one-to-one, one-to-many, many-to-many, et al. — between the objects that the software architects are great at defining.

With the new scenarios and problems at hand for the new applications, specifically for web or mobile-based social applications with a lot of user generated content, people realized that NoSQL databases would be a stronger fit than RDBMS databases.

In this chapter, we explore the traditional approach towards database, the challenges presented thereby, and the solutions provided by NoSQL for these challenges. We substantiate the ecosystem with a simple application as an example.

Application
ACME Foods is a grocery shop that wants to automate its inventory management. In this simplistic case, the process involves keeping an up-to-date status of its inventory and escalating to procurement, if levels are low.

RDBMS approach

The traditional approach—using RDBMS—takes the following route:

- **Identify actors**: The first step in the traditional approach is to identify various actors in the application. The actors can be internal or external to the application.

- **Define models**: Once the actors are identified, the next step is to create models. Typically, there is many-to-one mapping between actors and models, that is, one model may represent multiple actors.

- **Define entities**: Once the models and the object-relationships—by way of inheritance and encapsulation—are defined, the next step is to define the database entities. This requires defining the tables, columns, and column types. Special care has to be taken noting that databases allow null values for any column types, whereas programming languages may not allow, databases may have different size constraints as compared to really required, or a language allows, and much more.

- **Define relationships**: One of more important steps is to be able to well define the relationship between the entities. The only way to define relationships across tables is by using foreign keys. The entity relationships correspond to inheritance, one-to-one, one-to-many, many-to-many, and other object relationships.

- **Program database and application**: Once these are ready, engineers program database in PL/SQL (for most databases) or PL/pgSQL (for PostgreSQL) while software engineers develop the application.

- **Iterate**: Engineers may provide feedback to the architects and designers about the existing limitations and required enhancements in the models, entities, and relationships.

Mapping the steps to our example as follows:

- Few of the actors identified include buyer, employee, purchaser, administrator, office address, shipping address, supplier address, item in inventory, and supplier.

- They may be mapped to a model `UserProfile` and there may be subclasses as required—`Administrator` and `PointOfSalesUser`. Some of the other models include `Department`, `Role`, `Product`, `Supplier`, `Address`, `PurchaseOrder`, and `Invoice`.

- Simplistically, a database table may map each actor to a model.

- Foreign keys will be used to define the object relationships—one-to-many between `Department` and `UserProfile`, `many-to-many` between `Role` and `UserProfile`, and `PurchaseOrder` and `Product`.
- One would need simple SQL queries to access basic information while queries collating data across tables will need complex JOINs.
- Based on the inputs received later in time, one or more of these may need to be updated. New models and entities may evolve over time.

At a high level, the following entities and their relationships can be identified:

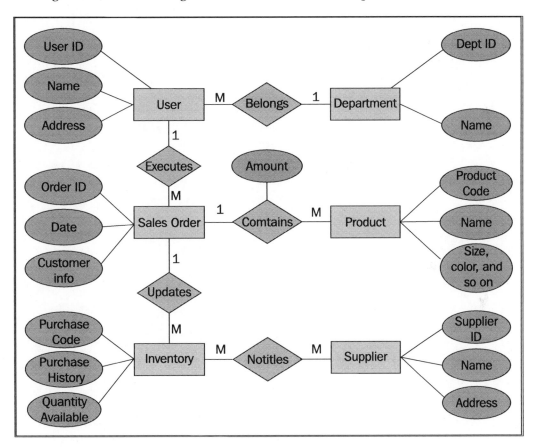

A department contains one or more users. A user may execute one or more sales orders each of which contains one or more products and updates the inventory. Items in inventory are provided by suppliers, which are notified if inventory level drops below critical levels. Representational class diagram may be closer to the one shown in the next figure:

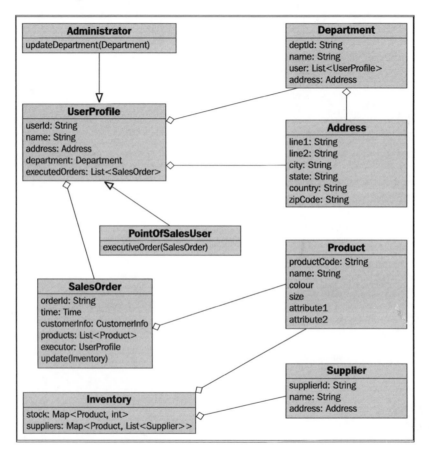

 These actors, models, entities, and relationships are only representative. In the real application, the definitions will be more elaborate and relationships more dense.

Let us take a quick look at the code that will take us there.

To start with, the models may shape as follows:

```
class UserProfile {
    int _id;
    UserType type;
    String firstName;
    String lastName;
    Department department;
    Collection<Role> roles;
    Address homeAddress;
    Address officeAddress;
}

class Address {
    String _id;
    String line1;
    String line2;
    String city;
    Country country;
    String zipCode;
}

enum Country {
    Australia, Bahrain, Canada, India, USA
}
```

The SQL statements used to create the tables for the previous models are:

```
CREATE TABLE Address(
    _id INT NOT NULL AUTO_INCREMENT,
    line1 VARCHAR(64) NOT NULL,
    line2 VARCHAR(64),
    city VARCHAR(32) NOT NULL,
    country VARCHAR(24) NOT NULL, /* Can be normalized */
    zipCode VARCHAR(8) NOT NULL,
    PRIMARY_KEY (_id)
);
```

```
CREATE TABLE UserProfile(
   _id INT NOT NULL AUTO_INCREMENT,
   firstName VARCHAR(32) NOT NULL,
   lastName VARCHAR(32) NOT NULL DEFAULT '',
   departmentId INT NOT NULL,
   homeAddressId INT NOT NULL,
   officeAddressId INT NOT NULL,
   PRIMARY_KEY (_id),
   FOREIGN_KEY (officeAddressId) REFERENCES Address(_id),
   FOREIGN_KEY (homeAddressId) REFERENCES Address(_id)
);
```

 The previous definitions are only representative but give an idea of what it requires to work in RDMBS world.

Challenges

The aforementioned approach sounds great, however, it has a set of challenges. Let us explore some of the possibilities that ACME Foods has or may encounter in future:

- The technical team faces a churn and key people maintaining the database—schema, programmability, business continuity process a.k.a. availability, and other aspects—leave. The company has a new engineering team and, irrespective of its expertise, has to quickly ramp up with existing entities, relationships, and code to maintain.

- The company wishes to expand their web presence and enable online orders. This requires either creating new user-related entities or enhancing the current entities.

- The company acquires another company and now needs to integrate the two database systems. This means refining models and entities. Critically, the database table relationships have to be carefully redefined.

- The company grows big and has to handle hundreds of millions of queries a day across the country. More so, it receives a few million orders. To scale, it has tied up with thousands of suppliers across locations and must provide away to integrate the systems.

- The company ties up with a few or several customer facing companies and intends to supply services to them to increase their sales. For this, it must integrate with multiple systems and also ensure that its application must be able to scale up to the combined needs of these companies, especially when multiple simultaneous orders are received in depleting inventory.

- The company plans to provide API integration for aggregators to retrieve and process their data. More importantly, it must ensure that the API must be forward compatible meaning that in future if it plans to change their internal database schema for whatever reasons, it must—if at all—minimally impact the externally facing API and schema for data-exchange.

- The company plans to leverage social networking sites, such as Facebook, Twitter, and FourSquare. For this, it seeks to not only use the simple widgets provided but also gather, monitor, and analyze statistics gathered.

The preceding functional requirements can be translated into the following technical requirements as far as the database is concerned:

- **Schema flexibility**: This will be needed during future enhancements and integration with external applications —outbound or inbound. RDBMS are quite inflexible in their design.

  More often than not, adding a column is an absolute no-no, especially if the table has some data and the reason lies in the constraint of having a default value for the new column and that the existing rows, by default, will have that default value. As a result you have to scan through the records and update the values as required, even if it can be automated. It may not be complex always, but frowned upon especially when the number of rows is large or number of columns to add is sufficiently large. You end up creating new tables and increase complexity by introducing relationships across the tables.

- **Complex queries**: Traditionally, the tables are designed denormalized which means that the developers end up writing complex so-called JOIN queries which are not only difficult to implement and maintain but also take substantial database resources to execute.

- **Data update**: Updating data across tables is probably one of the more complex scenarios especially if they are to be a part of the transaction. Note that keeping the transaction open for a long duration hampers the performance.

  One also has to plan for propagating the updates to multiple nodes across the system. And if the system does not support multiple masters or writing to multiple nodes simultaneously, there is a risk of node-failure and the entire application moving to read-only mode.

- **Scalability**: More often than not, the only scalability that may be required is for read operations. However, several factors impact this speed as operations grow. Some of the key questions to ask are:

  ° What is the time taken to synchronize the data across physical database instances?

  ° What is the time taken to synchronize the data across datacenters?

  ° What is the bandwidth requirement to synchronize data? Is the data exchanged optimized?

  ° What is the latency when any update is synchronized across servers? Typically, the records will be locked during an update.

NoSQL approach

NoSQL-based solutions provide answers to most of the challenges that we put up. Note that if ACME Grocery is very confident that it will not shape up as we discussed earlier, we *do not need NoSQL*. If ACME Grocery does not intend to grow, integrate, or provide integration with other applications, surely, the RDBMS will suffice. But that is not how anyone would like the business to work in the long term.

So, at some point in time, sooner or later, these questions will arise.

Let us see what NoSQL has to offer against each technical question that we have:

- **Schema flexibility**: Column-oriented databases (`http://en.wikipedia.org/wiki/Column-oriented_DBMS`) store data as columns as opposed to rows in RDBMS. This allows flexibility of adding one or more columns as required, on the fly. Similarly, document stores that allow storing semi-structured data are also good options.

- **Complex queries**: NoSQL databases do not have support for relationships or foreign keys. There are no complex queries. There are no `JOIN` statements.

  Is that a drawback? How does one query across tables?

  It is a functional drawback, definitely. To query across tables, multiple queries must be executed. Database is a shared resource, used across application servers and must not be released from use as quickly as possible.

  The options involve combination of simplifying queries to be executed, caching data, and performing complex operations in application tier.

A lot of databases provide in-built entity-level caching. This means that as and when a record is accessed, it may be automatically cached transparently by the database. The cache may be in-memory distributed cache for performance and scale.

- **Data update**: Data update and synchronization across physical instances are difficult engineering problems to solve.

  Synchronization across nodes within a datacenter has a different set of requirements as compared to synchronizing across multiple datacenters. One would want the latency within a couple of milliseconds or tens of milliseconds at the best. NoSQL solutions offer great synchronization options.

  MongoDB (`http://www.mongodb.org/display/DOCS/ Sharding+Introduction`), for example, allows concurrent updates across nodes (`http://www.mongodb.org/display/DOCS/ How+does+concurrency+work`), synchronization with conflict resolution and eventually, consistency across the datacenters within an acceptable time that would run in few milliseconds. As such, MongoDB has no concept of isolation.

  Note that now because the complexity of managing the transaction may be moved out of the database, the application will have to do some hard work. An example of this is a two-phase commit while implementing transactions (`http://docs.mongodb.org/manual/tutorial/ perform-two-phase-commits/`).

  Do not worry or get scared. A plethora of databases offer **Multiversion concurrency control (MCC)** to achieve transactional consistency (`http://en.wikipedia.org/wiki/Multiversion_concurrency_control`).

  Surprisingly, eBay does not use transactions at all (`http://www.infoq.com/ interviews/dan-pritchett-ebay-architecture`). Well, as Dan Pritchett (`http://www.addsimplicity.com/`), Technical Fellow at eBay puts it, eBay.com does not use transactions. Note that PayPal does use transactions.

- **Scalability**: NoSQL solutions provider greater scalability for obvious reasons. A lot of complexity that is required for transaction oriented RDBMS does not exist in ACID non-compliant NoSQL databases.

  Interestingly, since NoSQL do not provide cross-table references and there are no `JOIN` queries possible, and because one cannot write a single query to collate data across multiple tables, one simple and logical solution is to—at times—duplicate the data across tables. In some scenarios, embedding the information within the primary entity—especially in one-to-one mapping cases—may be a great idea.

Revisiting our earlier case of `Address` and `UserProfile`, if we use the document store, we can use JSON format to structure the data so that we do not need cross-table queries at all.

An example of how the data may look like is given as follows:

```
//UserProfile

{
   "_id": "98ef65e7-52e4-4466-bacc-3a8dc0c15c79",
   "firstName": "Gaurav",
   "lastName": "Vaish",
   "department": "f0adcbf5-7389-4491-9c42-f39a9d3d4c75",
   "homeAddress": {
      "_id": "fa62fd39-17f8-4a16-80d6-71a5b71d758d",
      "line1": "123, 45th Main",
      "city" : "NoSQLLand",
      "country": "India",
      "zipCode": "123456"
   }
}
```

 We explore various NoSQL database classes — based on data models provided — in *Chapter 3, NoSQL Storage Types*.

It is not that the new companies start with NoSQL straightaway. One can start with RDBMS and migrate to NoSQL — just keep in mind that it is not going to be trivial. Or better still, start with NoSQL. Even better, start with a mix of RDBMS and NoSQL. As we will see later, there are scenarios where it may be best to have a mix of the two databases.

A big case in consideration here is that of Netflix. The company moved from Oracle RDBMS to Apache Cassandra (`http://www.slideshare.net/hluu/netflix-moving-to-cloud`), and they could achieve over a million writes per second. Yes! That is 1,000,000 writes per second (`http://techblog.netflix.com/2011/11/benchmarking-cassandra-scalability-on.html`) across the cluster with over 10,000 writes per second per node while maintaining the average latency at less than 0.015 milliseconds! And the total cost of setting it all up and running on Amazon EC2 Cloud was at around $60 per hour — not per node but for a cluster of 48 nodes. Per node cost is only $1.25 per hour inclusive of the storage capacity of 12.8 Terra-bytes, network read bandwidth of 22 Mbps, and write bandwidth of 18.6Mbps.

The preceding case-in-hand should not undermine the power of and features provided by Oracle RDBMS database. I have always considered it as one of the best commercial solutions available in RDBMS space.

Summary

In this chapter we explored key characteristics of NoSQL and what they have to offer in depth vis-à-vis RDBMS databases.

We looked at typical approach used while working with and the challenges at hand when dealing with traditional RDMBS approach. We also looked how a large set of functional requirement lead to structured, small set of technical problems and how NoSQL databases solve these problems.

It is important to note that NoSQL is not a solution to all the problems that one will ever come across while working with RDBMS though it does provide answers to most of questions. Having said that, NoSQL may not be the ideal solution in specific cases, especially in financial applications where what matters is immediate and momentous consistency and not mere eventual consistency.

In the next chapter, we will explore various data models available in NoSQL databases.

3
NoSQL Storage Types

Great. At this point, we have a very good understanding of what NoSQL databases have to offer and what challenges they solve.

The NoSQL databases are categorized on the basis of how the data is stored. Because of the need to provide curated information from large volumes, generally in near real-time, NoSQL mostly follows a horizontal structure. They are optimized for insert and retrieve operations on a large scale with built-in capabilities for replication and clustering. Some of the functionalities of SQL databases like functions, stored procedures, and PL may not be present in most of the databases.

In this chapter, we explore various storage types provided by these databases, comparing and contrasting them, and more critically identifying what to use when.

This chapter refers to several commonly understood standards and rules used today with RDBMS; for example table schema, CRUD operations, JOIN, VIEW, and a few more.

Storage types

There are various storage types available in which the content can be modeled for NoSQL databases. In subsequent sections, we will explore the following storage types:

- Column-oriented
- Document Store
- Key Value Store
- Graph

Column-oriented databases

The column-oriented databases store data as columns as opposed to rows that is prominent in RDBMS. The details can be found at `http://www.scribd.com/doc/92371275/Column-Oriented-DB-Systems` and `http://dbmsmusings.blogspot.in/2009/09/tour-through-hybrid-columnrow-oriented.html`.

 Column stores have been in development since early DBMS days. TAXIR, a biology information-retrieval-focused application, was the first application using column-oriented stores way back in 1969.

A relational database shows the data as two-dimensional tables comprising of rows and columns but stores, retrieves, and processes it one row at a time, whereas a column-oriented database stores data as columns.

For example, assume that the following data is to be stored:

EmployeeID	FirstName	LastName	Age	Salary
SM1	Anuj	Sharma	45	10000000
MM2	Anand		34	5000000
T3	Vikas	Gupta	39	7500000
E4	Dinesh	Verma	32	2000000

In RDBMS, the data may be serialized and stored internally as follows:

```
SM1,Anuj,Sharma,45,10000000
MM2,Anand,,34,5000000
T3,Vikas,Gupta,39,7500000
E4,Dinesh,Verma,32,2000000
```

However, in column-oriented databases, the data will be stored internally as follows:

```
SM1,MM2,T3,E4
Anuj,Anand,Vikas,Dinesh
Sharma,,Gupta,Verma,
45,34,39,32
10000000,5000000,7500000,2000000
```

The preceding representation is over simplified. Databases typically will have more sophisticated and optimized mechanisms to store data. Tasks like partitioning, caching, indexing, and ability to create OLAP cubes, and others affect the underlying physical organization of the data within the system.

Online transaction processing (OLTP) focused relational databases are row oriented. **Online analytical processing (OLAP)** systems that require processing of data need column-oriented access. Having said that, OLTP operations may also require column-oriented access when working on a subset of columns and operating on them.

Data access to these databases is typically done by using either a proprietary protocol in case of commercial solutions or open standard binary (for example, **Remote Method Invocation**). The transport protocol is generally binary.

Some of the databases that fall under this category include:

- Oracle RDBMS Columnar Expression
- Microsoft SQL Server 2012 Enterprise Edition
- Apache Cassandra
- HBase
- Google BigTable (available as part of Google App Engine branded Datastore)

Advantages

Most of the solutions, such as Apache Cassandra, HBase, and Google Datastore, allow adding columns over time without having to worry about filling in default values for the existing rows for the new columns. This gives flexibility in model and entity design allowing one to account for new columns in future for unforeseen scenarios and new requirements.

There are advantages when working with a subset of the available columns. For example, computing maxima, minima, averages and sums, specifically on large datasets, is where these column-oriented data stores outshine in performance.

Similarly, when new values are applied for either all rows at once or with same-column filters, these databases will allow partial data access without touching unrelated columns and be much faster in execution.

Since columns will be of uniform type and mostly (except in cases of variable-length strings) of the same length, there are possibilities of efficient storage in terms of size. Such as a column with the same values across rows (for example, the department of a user profile or whether a user's profile is public or private or even a user's age), the same or similar adjacent values can be compressed efficiently.

Example

In the following example, you will find sample code for working with Google's Datastore (can be found at `https://developers.google.com/appengine/docs/java/datastore/`) on Google App Engine using the Objectify (`http://code.google.com/p/objectify-appengine/`) library:

```
public class UserProfile
{
   @Id String employeeID;
   String firstName;
   String lastName;
   String age;
   long salary;
}

ObjectifyService.register(UserProfile.class);
Objectify ofy = ObjectifyService.begin();

//Adding records

UserProfile up1 = new UserProfile(...);
UserProfile up2 = new UserProfile(...);

ofy.put(up1, up2);

//Retrieve by Id

UserProfile upg = ofy.get(UserProfile.class, "SM1");

//Filter all profiles by first name

Iterator<UserProfile> profiles
    = ofy.query(UserProfile.class)
         .filter("firstName", "Alice");
```

```
//Query all profiles by age greater than 30, ordered by salary

Iterator<UserProfile> agedProfiles
    = ofy.query(UserProfile.class)
        .filter("age >", 30)
        .order("salary");
```

Document store

Also referred to as document-oriented database, a document store allows the inserting, retrieving, and manipulating of semi-structured data. Most of the databases available under this category use XML, JSON, BSON, or YAML, with data access typically over HTTP protocol using RESTful API or over Apache Thrift protocol for cross-language interoperability.

Compared to RDBMS, the documents themselves act as records (or rows), however, it is semi-structured as compared to rigid RDBMS.

For example, two records may have completely different set of fields or columns. The records may or may not adhere to a specific schema (like the table definitions in RDBMS). For that matter, the database may not support a schema or validating a document against the schema at all.

Even though the documents do not follow a strict schema, indexes can be created and queried. Here are some examples of document content using JSON:

One document may provide an employee whose whole details are not completely known:

```
{
    "EmployeeID": "SM1",
    "FirstName" : "Anuj",
    "LastName"  : "Sharma",
    "Age"       : 45,
    "Salary"    : 10000000
}
```

A second document may have complete details about another employee:

```
{
    "EmployeeID": "MM2",
    "FirstName" : "Anand",
    "Age"       : 34,
    "Salary"    : 5000000,
    "Address"   : {
```

```
        "Line1"    : "123, 4th Street",
        "City"     : "Bangalore",
        "State"    : "Karnataka"
      },
      "Projects"   : [
        "nosql-migration",
        "top-secret-007"
      ]
  }
```

A third document may have information about one of the office locations:

```
  {
      "LocationID"          : "Bangalore-SDC-BTP-CVRN",
      "RegisteredName"      : "ACME Software Development Ltd"
      "RegisteredAddress" : {
        "Line1"      : "123, 4th Street",
        "City"       : "Bangalore",
        "State"      : "Karnataka"
      },
  }
```

If you notice the preceding examples, the first two documents are somewhat similar with the second document having more details as compared to the first. However, if you look at the third document, the content has no correlation to the first two documents whatsoever — this is about an office location rather than an employee.

The `EmployeeID` or `LocationID` may not be the document ID. The databases provide access using RESTful APIs wherein the document ID is part of the URL itself or is provided within the body of the request. Having said that, it is not mandatory that the document content should not contain its ID. In fact, one of the best practices states that the document ID must be embedded in the document somewhere and preferably in a standard location. For example, the modified content may be:

```
  {
    "docId": "SM1",
    ...
  }


  {
    "docId": "MM2",
    ...
  }


  {
    "docId": "Bangalore-SDC-BTP-CVRN",
    ...
  }
```

Document-oriented databases provide this flexibility—dynamic or changeable schema or even schemaless documents. Because of the limitless flexibility provided in this model, this is one of the more popular models implemented and used.

Some of popular databases that provide document-oriented storage include:

- MongoDB
- CouchDB
- Jackrabbit
- Lotus Notes
- Apache Cassandra
- Terrastore
- Redis
- BaseX

Advantages

The most prominent advantage, as evident in the preceding examples, is that content is schemaless, or at best loosely defined. This is very useful in web-based applications where there is a need for storing different types of content that may evolve over time. For example, for a grocery store, information about the users, inventory and orders can be stored as simple JSON or XML documents. Note that "document store" is not the same as "blob store" where the data cannot be indexed.

Based on the implementation, it may or may not be possible to retrieve or update a record partially. If it is possible to do so, there is a great advantage. Note that stores based on XML, BSON, JSON, and YAML would typically support this. XML-based BaseX can be really powerful, while integrating multiple systems working with XML given that it supports XQuery 3.0 and XSLT 2.0.

Searching across multiple entity types is far more trivial compared to doing so in traditional RDBMS or even in column-oriented databases. Because, now, there is no concept of tables—which is essentially nothing more than a schema definition—one can query across the records, irrespective of the underlying content or schema or in other words, the query is directly against the entire database. Note that the databases allow for the creation of indexes (using common parameters or otherwise and evolve over time).

JSON-based stores are easy to define what I call **projections**. Each top-level key for the JSON object may be the entity's projection across other parts of the system thereby allowing the schema to evolve over time with backward compatibility.

Examples

To start with, let us have a look at a JSON-based document demonstrating the advantages that we just discussed:

```
{
  "me": {
    "id"          : "document-uuid",
    "version"     : "1.0.0.0",
    "create_time" : "2011-11-11T11:11:11Z",
    "last_update" : "2012-12-12T12:12:12Z"
  },
  "type": "UserProfile",
  "personal": {
    "firstName" : "Alice",
    "lastName"  : "Matthews",
    "date_of_birth": "1901-01-01T01:01:01Z"
  },
  "financial": {
    "bank"           : { ... },
    "trading"        : { ... },
    "credit-history" : { ... }
  },
  "criminal": {
  }
}
```

The document structure has been carefully designed as the following:

- The me attribute is the basic information about the record. It comprises the unique id of the document which never changes, version that must be updated each time the record changes, creation_time marking when the record was created, and last_update indicating when the record was last updated. This can be mandatory for sanity.

- The type attribute specifies the entity type represented in this document. This, again, can be made mandatory.

- Other attributes such as personal, financial, criminal, and few more can be added over time.

- It is these attributes that I refer to as projections that provide context-specific data. These contexts don't need to be initially defined and generally evolve over time. The advantage, as we see, is that all the data associated with the entity resides in one record—the document—and redundancy can help speeding up the queries.

- Databases like MongoDB allow to the creation of schemaless entities so that one can get rid of the `type` attribute and support views that can be used to query across various entity types similar to what `JOIN` does in SQL.

The next example demonstrates the use of JSON with CouchDB and how these concepts can be put into action. Since CouchDB has no concept of tables and anything that you add is a simple, unstructured but legal JSON document, we keep the document the same as before and concentrate on how and what operations can be performed on the data.

CouchDB provides a RESTful HTTP interface with the standard HTTP methods mapping to the data operations—**GET** (retrieve), **POST** (create or update, implicit / implied ID), **PUT** (create or update, explicit/specified ID), **DELETE** (delete). We assume that the CouchDB HTTP server is up and running on `localhost` at default port 5984.

We will explore CRUD operations along with basic database operations. For ease of operations, we use the command line program curl (`http://curl.haxx.se/docs/manpage.html`) to execute the HTTP requests. Notice how CouchDB makes use of the ID, revision, and looseness in schema:

1. Creating a database named `ShoppingDB`:

   ```
   curl -X PUT http://localhost:5984/ShoppingDB
   ```

   You will get the following response:

   ```
   { "ok": true }
   ```

2. Get a summary of the database:

   ```
   curl http://localhost:5984/ShoppingDB
   {
       "db_name"   : "ShoppingDB"
       "doc_count": 0
       // Removed other attributes for brevity
   }
   ```

3. Assuming that the content is stored in the `data.json` file, adding the document to the store using `document-uuid` as the ID as provided in the document. Technically speaking, the `document-uuid` can be any unique identifier—as simple as `123`.

It is important to note that, if not provided, MongoDB automatically generates an ID for each document inserted. The field name is _id.

```
curl -X PUT -H "Content-Type: application/json" \
    http://localhost:5984/ShoppingDB/document-uuid \
    -d @data.json
```

You will get the following response:

```
{
  "ok": true,
  "id": "document-uuid",
  "rev": "1-Revision-UUID"
}
```

4. Retrieving the document:

```
curl http://localhost:5984/ShoppingDB/document-uuid
```

You will get the following response:

```
{
  "_id": "document-uuid",
  "_rev": "1-Revision-UUID",
  "me": {
    "id": "document-uuid",
    ...
  }
  ...
}
```

The remaining document was removed for brevity. The content is nothing but whatever was inserted.

5. Update the document. Note that the revision that is being updated is required and that it has been updated:

```
curl -X PUT -H "Content-Type: text/json" \
    http://localhost:5984/ShoppingDB/document-uuid
    -d '{ "name": "Alice Taylor", "_rev": "1-Revision-UUID" }'
```

You will get the following response:

```
{
    "ok": true,
    "id": "document-uuid",
    "rev": "2-Revision-UUID"
}
```

6. Deleting the document is as simple as executing a DELETE method on the document ID:

    ```
    curl -X DELETE http://localhost:5984/ShoppingDB/document-uuid
    ```

    You will get the following response:

    ```
    { "ok": true }
    ```

7. These were simple operations, and looked mostly trivial. The fun and unleashing power starts when, for example, one needs to execute a — probably hypothetical — query to fetch all documents across the database that has an attribute title or expertise that contains NoSQL without worrying about the capitalization. Let title be a simple string and expertise be an array in the JSON document.

    The case in hand is profiles may have their technical expertise listed or there may be a company whose name contains the string.

    This — we know — is quite a daunting task in any database that has the notion of tables because then searching across tables and then presenting in a unified manner is next to impossible. However theoretical or hypothetical this query may be, it demonstrates the power behind such an implementation of NoSQL database.

    CouchDB does support views and the output of the view is also a JSON document with the language for implementing the logic to define the view is JavaScript and the functions are referred to as **map and reduce functions** (http://en.wikipedia.org/wiki/Mapreduce). The function takes the document (JSON object) as a parameter and *emits* out a JSON object representing the output of the view and a unique ID to identify the record (can be any valid JavaScript type).

The map function emits out the value that will be consumed by the reduce function (we use the document ID as the ID of the record returned):

```
function(doc) {
  var pattern = /nosql/i;
  if(pattern.test(doc.title)) {
    emit(doc['_id'], doc);
  } else if(doc.expertise && doc.expertise.length) {
    pattern = /,nosql,/i;
    if(pattern.test(',' + doc.expertise.join(',') + ',')) {
      emit(doc['_id'], doc);
    }
  }
}
```

The reduce function gives the final data that can be consumed in the business application layer. Following are some reduce functions:

- Returns the complete document:

```
function(key, value, rereduce) {
  return value;
}
```

- Returns the id and address attribute from the document:

```
function(key, value, rereduce) {
  return {
    "_id": value["_id"],
    "address": value["address"]
  };
}
```

- Returns all attributes other than the address attribute:

```
function(key, value, rereduce) {
  delete value.address;
  return value;
}
```

The next example demonstrates using JSON with MongoDB that allows segregation of records using the notion of collections (similar to tables in SQL). MongoDB, interestingly, does not need a database to be created before data insertion is done. As the official documentation reads:

> *... MongoDB does not require that you do so* **(create a database)**. *As soon as you insert something, MongoDB creates the underlying collection* **(similar to databases in RDBMS world)** *and database. If you query a collection that does not exist, MongoDB treats it as an empty collection* **(means, you never get errors)**. *(Found at* `http://www.mongodb.org/display/DOCS/Tutorial`*).*

The emphasis is mine.

Since MongoDB does not provide RESTful interface over HTTP out of the box, we execute the code on the MongoDB console.

8. Even though not mandatory, here is how to create a collection:

    ```
    > db.createCollection("userprofile");
    ```

9. Inserting a record into `userprofile` collection (document stripped for brevity):

 Note that the document does not contain the `type` attribute since MongoDB supports the notion of collection, which is nothing but `type`.

```
> db.userprofile.insert({
    "me": {
      "id": "document-uuid",
      ...
    },
    "personal": {
      "firstName": "Alice",
      ...
    }
});
```

 While working with MongoDB, it is always a good idea to have the record ID in the document itself, like for our case it is `me` => `id`.

10. To update a record, use the `update` method that expects two arguments. The first argument is a query to filter the record to be updated. The second argument provides details about the updated values. These steps are similar to that in SQL for an UPDATE statement where the first argument is similar to the WHERE clause and the second argument similar to the SET clause:

```
> db.userprofile.update( {
    "me.id": "uuid-to-search-for"
  }, {
    "$set": {
      "personal.lastName": "Taylor"
    }
  }
);
```

 Notice that MongoDB treats dot (.) as a separator to traverse within the object. As such, it is advisable not to use dot in attribute names.

Treat `firstName` as a legal attribute while `name.first` as an attribute name to be avoided.

11. To retrieve records, we can use any of the attributes:

```
> db.userprofile.find( {
    "personal.firstName": "Bob"
  }
);
```

12. To delete a record or records, all that is required is to be able to query for appropriate attribute or attributes. For example, to remove profiles whose age is greater than 30 and the city of thier personal address is Madrid:

```
> db.userprofile.remove({
    "personal.age": { $gt: 30 },
    "personal.address.city": "Madrid"
  }
);
```

13. After exploring some of these basic operations, let us get into some complex, real-world scenarios of querying the data, configuring specific indexes, and returning partial document.

To start with, let us reintroduce the problem that we discussed earlier while dealing with CouchDB, that is, querying for "NoSQL" in `title` as well as `expertise`, and look at the solution that MongoDB has to offer. Additionally, now that we understand that the collection—`userprofile`—is merely a collection of documents, we can safely rename it to `shoppingDB` for incorporating the larger scope that we operate with in subsequent examples:

```
> db.shoppingDB.find( {
    $or: [
      { "title": /NoSql/i },
      { "expertise": /NoSql/i }
    ]
  }
);
```

In another scenario, let us assume that profiles have `sales`—an array of objects corresponding to monthly sales since the time the user joined the company with each object having information about the month and sales figures. What we want to query is all the profiles that cross the sales of 500,000 in their first month of joining:

```
//Sample document
{
    "me": { ... },
    "sales": [ { "month": 201201", "value": 100000 }, ...]
}

//The query

> db.shoppingDB.find({
    "sales.0.value >= ": 500000
  }
);
```

If you notice in the query the first argument to the `find` method, you notice a strange syntax—`sales.0.value`. The interpretation is, for the array `sales`, take the item at index `0` and for that item, pickup the value for the property value, and if the value if greater than or equal to `500000`, select the item. For complete details on dot notation in query, have a look at `http://docs.mongodb.org/manual/core/document/#dot-notation`.

Let us now explore the other side of the query—the results. So far whatever we searched for, we received the complete documents. Let us take some cases where we need only a part of the document—similar to creating a view in CouchDB. To do so, we make use of the optional second parameter wherein we can specify the document fragment to be included or excluded.

In the first case, we select only `personal => firstName` and `sales`:

```
> db.shoppingDB.find( { ... }, {
    "personal.firstName": 1,
    "sales": 1
  }
);
```

In the next case, we select all fields except `criminal` record:

```
> db.shoppingDB.find( { ... }, {
    "criminal": 0
  }
);
```

In the last case, we select only the last five sales elements across all the documents (cool!):

```
> db.shoppingDB.find( { }, {
    "sales": { $slice: -5 }
  }
);
```

 Note that even though MongoDB supports collections, it does not enforce restrictions on the schema. This essentially means that MongoDB is akin to having multiple instances of CouchDB running under a single umbrella.

Key-value store

A **Key-value store** is very closely related to a document store—it allows the storage of a value against a key. Similar to a document store, there is no need for a schema to be enforced on the value. However, there a are few constraints that are enforced by a key-value store (`http://ayende.com/blog/4459/that-no-sql-thing-document-databases`):

- Unlike a document store that can create a key when a new document is inserted, a key-value store requires the key to be specified

- Unlike a document store where the value can be indexed and queried, for a key-value store, the value is opaque and as such, the key must be known to retrieve the value

If you are familiar with the concept of maps or associative arrays (`http://en.wikipedia.org/wiki/Associative_array`) or have worked with hash tables (`http://en.wikipedia.org/wiki/Hash_table`), then you already have worked with a in-memory key-value store.

The most prominent use of working with a key-value store is for in-memory distributed or otherwise cache. However, implementations do exist to provide persistent storage.

A few of the popular key value stores are:

- **Redis** (in-memory, with dump or command-log persistence)
- **Memcached** (in-memory)
- **MemcacheDB** (built on Memcached)
- **Berkley DB**
- **Voldemort** (open source implementation of Amazon Dynamo)

Advantages

Key-value stores are optimized for querying against keys. As such, they serve great in-memory caches. Memcached and Redis support expiry for the keys—sliding or absolute—after which the entry is evicted from the store.

At times, one can generate the keys smartly—say, bucketed UUID—and can query against ranges of keys. For example, Redis allows retrieving a list of all the keys matching a glob-style pattern.

While the time complexity for this operation (search for keys matching a pattern) is O(N), the constant times are fairly low. For example, Redis running on an entry level laptop can scan a 1 million key database in 40 milliseconds. (source found at http://redis.io/commands/keys).

Though the key-value stores cannot query on the values, they can still understand the type of value. Stores like Redis support different value types—strings, hashes, lists, sets, and sorted sets. Based on the value types, advanced functionalities can be provided. Some of them include atomic increment, setting/updating multiple fields of a hash (equivalent of partially updating the document), and intersection, union, and difference while working with sets.

Examples

Let us explore some basic data operations using the Redis (http://redis.io database). Note that there is no concept of database or table in Redis:

- Set or update value against a key:

```
SET company "My Company"          //String
HSET alice firstName "Alice"      //Hash - set field value
HSET alice lastName "Matthews"    //Hash - set field value
LPUSH "alice:sales" "10" "20"     //List create/append
LSET "alice:sales" "0" "4"        //List update
SADD "alice:friends" "f1" "f2"    //Set - create/update
SADD "bob:friends" "f2" "f1"      //Set - create/update
```

Having done that, let us explore some interesting operations on sets and lists:

- Set operations:

```
//Intersection - Get mutual friends of Alice and Bob
SINTER "alice:friends" "bob:friends"

//Difference - Friends in Alice's list absent in Bob's
SDIFF "alice:friends" "bob:friends"

//Union - All friends that need invitation in their marriage
SUNION "alice:friends" "bob:friends"
```

- List operations:

```
//Pop the first item, or return null

POP "key:name"

//Blocking pop - pop the first item, or wait until timeout or next
is available (check across lists - l1, l2, l3)

BLPOP l1 l2 l3

//Pop item from list1, append to list2 and return the value

RPOPLPUSH list1 list2
```

> Key-value stores are not designed for applications that need indexes on the values. Because of optimization on key-queries, implementations like Memcached or Redis are great candidates for distributed, scalable, in-memory cache.

Graph store

Graph databases represent a special category of NoSQL databases where relationships are represented as graphs. There can be multiple links between two nodes in a graph—representing the multiple relationships that the two nodes share.

The relationships represented may include social relationships between people, transport links between places, or network topologies between connected systems.

Graphical representation of a graph may look similar to the following graph
(`http://docs.neo4j.org/chunked/milestone/what-is-a-graphdb.html`):

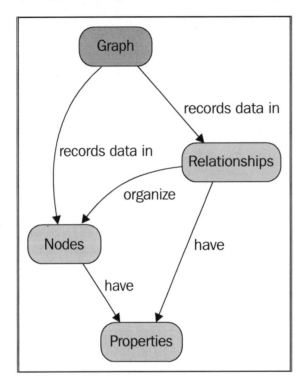

Graph databases are fairly new in the market with only a few proven solutions
out there:

- Neo4j
- FlockDB (from Twitter)

Advantages

An article found at `http://www.infoq.com/articles/graph-nosql-neo4j` quotes
the advantages as follows:

> *Graph theory has seen a great usefulness and relevance in many problems across
> various domains. The most applied graph theoretic algorithms include various
> types of shortest path calculations, geodesic paths, centrality measures like
> PageRank, eigenvector centrality, closeness, betweenness, HITS, and many others.*

Graph databases can be considered as special purpose NoSQL databases optimized for relation-heavy data. If there is no relationship among the entities, there is no usecase for graph databases.

The one advantage that graph databases have is easy representation, retrieval and manipulation of relationships between the entities in the system.

It is not uncommon to store data in a document store and relationships in a graph database.

Examples

The following code demonstrates how to create a simple relationship between two nodes with Neo4J:

```
//Assume that we get the underlying database service somehow
GraphDatabaseService db = ...

Node node1 = db.createNode();
node1.setProperty("documentId", "alice");

Node node2 = db.createNode();
node2.setProperty("documentId", "bob");

RelationType friendRel = new RelationType() {
    public String name() { return "friend"; }
};

Relationship reln = node1.createRelationshipTo(node2,
                                        friendRel);
reln.setProperty("initatedBy", "alice");
reln.setProperty("createdOn", "1980-01-01T07:30+0530");
```

The next example demonstrates how to retrieve all adjacent nodes against a relationship and pivot node:

```
//Define an index

Index<Node> nodeIndex = db.index().forNodes("nodes");

//While creating a node, add it to the index
nodeIndex.add(node1, "documentId",
                (String) node1.getProperty("documentId"));

//Search for a specific node
```

```
Node aliceNode = nodeIndex.get("documentId, "alice").single();

//Get all friend relationships
Iterable<Relationship> rels =
            aliceNode.getRelationships(friendRel);

//Get friends on the other side of the relationship

for(Relationship r: rels)
{
    Node friendNode = r.getEndNode();
    assert "bob".equals(friendNode.getProperty("documentId"))
}
```

 Use graph databases to store the relationships. Do not use them for complete data store; the performance may degrade. Neo4j is full ACID-compliant database—something that one may want while dealing with relationships.

Multi-storage type databases

Apart from the databases that we discussed earlier, following is a list of databases that support multiple storage types, giving you flexibility:

- **OrientDB**: Supports document store, key-value as well as graph. The official website is http://www.orientdb.org.

- **ArangoDB**: Universal database with support for document store, key-value and graph models. Official website is http://www.arangodb.org.

- **Aerospike**: A very interesting database that is a hybrid between RDBMS and NoSQL store. It supports document store, key-value, graph as well as RDBMS. Source code can be found at https://github.com/JakSprats/Alchemy-Database.

Comparing the models

Now that we have explored the popular storage or data models, let us compare them on key parameters of features:

Feature	Column Oriented	Document Store	Key Value Store	Graph
Table-like schema support (columns)	Yes	No	No	Yes
Complete update/ fetch	Yes	Yes	Yes	Yes
Partial update/ fetch	Yes	Yes	Yes	No
Query/Filter on value	Yes	Yes	No	Yes
Aggregates across rows	Yes	No	No	No
Relationships between entities	No	No	No	Yes
Cross-entity view support	No	Yes	No	No
Batch fetch	Yes	Yes	Yes	Yes
Batch update	Yes	Yes	Yes	No

Note that although we have Yes as well as No across the columns, the difference between the various models is getting blurred over time.

For example, a couple of years back the key-value stores would consider values are opaque blobs where as today they support granular query and update today.

Similarly, earlier document stores allowed ID-based CRUD operations but databases such as MongoDB support bulk updates today.

The key question is—what model to use in what scenario?

Well, if you have just landed from RDBMS world, modeling with column-oriented databases may give you quick hands-on experience with NoSQL modeling. One more real-world case is when you have more need to work with aggregate values as compared to individual values—for example, social-heavy applications. If you intend to work with the Google App Engine—well, you have no choice but to use this model. Facebook uses HBase to power their messages infrastructure while Yahoo! uses the same to store document fingerprint to detect near-duplications (`http://wiki.apache.org/hadoop/Hbase/PoweredBy`).

Document-oriented store systems are one type that can serve you across the application types including where you have a heavy need for aggregates across the entities. MapReduce-based implementations give you amazing control over querying the data such as working with JSON using nested properties, and with XML using XQuery; and creating response structures such as creating aggregates, and custom views across entity types. Companies like Facebook (HBase), Netflix, Twitter, and eBay (Cassandra) have given tremendous impetus to the evolution of document stores and it continues to lead the pack by a huge margin (`http://www.datastax.com/cassandrausers`).

Key-value stores are great options similar to document-oriented stores. The only missing feature is querying against the value. However, with time, this differentiation seems to be headed for blurriness. One case where key-value stores win hands-down is distributed in-memory cache. Extensive use of Memcached and Redis prove the same.

Graph databases are particularly useful in defining relationships across entities at database level as opposed to in other models where the relationships are only visible at application level. Twitter has open sourced FlockDB that it uses exclusively to store social graphs (`https://github.com/twitter/flockdb`).

However, if you are designing the database for the lightweight shopping application, the RDBMS approach is the perfect fit for the same.

Summary

In this chapter we discussed key data models available while working with NoSQL databases. We looked at some of the key features available with these models. These models, however, are not exhaustive. There are some other models also available:

- Object databases
- Multidimensional databases
- Multi-value databases

Last but not the least, we compared these models across some key parameters and looked at some common scenarios describing which model to use.

Although NoSQL databases are great, they may not always be a good choice always. In the next chapter we take a deeper dive, to identify what fits into which scenario.

4

Advantages and Drawbacks

Having understood the modeling options available in NoSQL along with the RDBMS knowledge that we already had, we are now in a position to understand the pros and cons of using NoSQL.

In this chapter, we will take three different representative application requirements and discuss advantages and disadvantages of using NoSQL, and conclude whether or not to use NoSQL in that specific scenario.

We will analyze by understanding the database requirements, identifying the advantages and drawbacks, and finally coming to a conclusion on NoSQL use as follows:

- **Entity schema requirements**: What is the density of relationships across entities, whether or not the schema change over time and if so, what is the frequency

- **Data access requirements**: Should the data be always consistent or can be eventually consistent (say, after 10 ms or 10 days or whatever), would the data access be more horizontal (row-wise) or vertical (column-wise)

- **What NoSQL can do**: What does NoSQL have to offer in the given scenario

- **What NoSQL cannot do**: Where NoSQL fails or leaves a lot of work to be done at the application tier in the given scenario.

- **Whether or not to use NoSQL**: If NoSQL is a good choice, which data model fits best with it.

At a broad level, I have classified the applications into the following categories:

- Relational-data driven, transaction-heavy applications

- Data-driven, computation-heavy applications

- Web-scale, data-driven applications where minor latencies are acceptable

Transactional application

This type of application has data that is highly relational in nature. Important application characteristics are:

- The application relies on the consistency and integrity of the data
- The concurrency (usage) is relatively lower
    - Lower is a relative adjective—all that we are looking for here is that the application can be served by a single database instance without any replication or load-balance requirements
    - It may choose to have mirrors or replication for automatic failover or otherwise but the application talks to a maximum of one instance—may switch over in case of failover

An example of this is the application at the point-of-sales at a grocery shop or an enterprise resource management application. The key here is data consistency.

Entity schema requirements

For a transactional application, general requirements for the entity schema include:

- Highly structured definition—properties, types, and constraints, if applicable
- Ability to define relationships—parent versus child keys
- Schema does not evolve or vary too much over time.

Data access requirements

From a data access perspective, we would have the following requirements:

- Consistency—any read should return latest updated data
- More often than not, the entire record (row) will be retrieved
- Cross-entity (table) data access may be frequent

What NoSQL can do

For a transactional application, NoSQL can help as follows:

- Column-oriented database helps define structure. If need be, it can be changed over time.
- Document-oriented database can help implement JOIN or create views.

What NoSQL cannot do

Using NoSQL will result in a few limitations for a transactional application:

- Inability to define relationships

- Absence of transactions (Neo4j is an exception)

- Unavailability of ACID properties in operations (CouchDB and Neo4j are the exceptions)

- Using Cassandra or CouchDB can be overkill if we compare them to, for example, MySQL or PostgreSQL — they do not unleash their true power in a single-machine installation

- Absence of support for JOIN and cross-entity query, though document-oriented stores support it by way of MapReduce but the efforts may be substantial as the queries get complex

Decision

Choose RDBMS rather than NoSQL. The disadvantages outweigh the advantages.

Computational application

This type of application does a lot of computation in the application. Key characteristics of this application type are:

- Most of the operations are along a given set of properties across the records

- The data stored may still be relational but the computation-centric data definitely has sparse relations, if any

An example of this type of application is a survey application or a sales record management application. The key here is that the computation is across the records but on a subset of the properties or columns available (the subset in an extreme case can be 100 percent of the available columns). Also, a survey application would require ability to define custom fields and operations.

Entity schema requirements

For a computational application, general requirements on the entity schema include:

- Structured schema definition — properties, types, and constraints, if applicable.

- Schema does not evolve or vary too much over time.

Data access requirements

From a data access perspective, we would have the following requirements:

- Partial record access.

- Vertical, that is, column-wise processing.

  For example, for an entity holding the data of daily revenues and expenses at a given location of operation, one would compute across the revenue column and/or expense column more often than working on the entire row.

- Cross-entity data access is infrequent.

  For example, to create the final balance sheet for a location, I may use the location ID once to get the details about the location.

- Consistency — data should be consistent. However, in some cases, minor latencies are allowed.

  For example, since the reports may be generated daily rather than in real-time, the user is happy working with day-old data.

What NoSQL can do

For a computational application, NoSQL can help as follows:

- Column-oriented databases would help define rigorous schema. Document or key-value databases can still be used.

  For example, JSON formats can be used to define a formal schema. Just that these stores cannot enforce the schema.

- They (column-oriented, key-value as well as document stores) can provide speed and scale while fetching partial data.

- Document stores coupled with MapReduce processing can help performing computation right up close to the data-tier thereby substantially increasing the speed of execution. You do not want unnecessary data to be floating across the network.

- Document stores can help implement JOIN or create views.

What NoSQL cannot do

Using NoSQL will result in a few limitations for a computational application:

- Defining relationships can be tricky. Except for graph databases, these relationships must be maintained in application.

- Because relationships do not exist in the database, data can be inconsistent—even if momentarily.

Decision

The list of tasks that are possible in NoSQL are also possible with RDBMS. The only brownie point that NoSQL gets here, which can turn out to be a big differentiator, is the speed and scale at which data can be partitioned horizontally and fetched property-wise.

RDBMS systems do allow the filtering of queries such as the one given in the following:

```
SELECT revenue, expense FROM location_finance WHERE location_id=1234
```

However, internally RDBMS systems are tuned to fetch the entire row at the time from the underlying physical store and then apply the filter—especially the columns selected using the SELECT statement.

On the other hand, NoSQL databases—especially column-oriented databases—are highly optimized to retrieve partial records and can result in a dramatic performance difference against RDBMS while dealing with hundreds of millions or billions of records.

To conclude, it is a tough choice between RDBMS and NoSQL databases in this case. If the application is, say, an enterprise application wherein the number of records will be limited to around, for example, a hundred million or lower, RDBMS can just serve it right, though NoSQL can also be used. For any size less than a million records, NoSQL can have overheads in terms of setup and tuning; while for over a few hundred million records, RDBMS will taper down in performance.

Web-scale application

This last application type is probably more relevant today in consumer applications, whether they are completely web-based or mobile-native apps or a combination of both.

Some of the key characteristics of this type of application are:

- The application should be able to scale because of the enormous volume of content that it operates on, the sheer number of users, and the vast geography where the users access it because of which one datacenter is unfeasible.

- The users of this application may be fine working with non-real-time, relatively stale data. The staleness may range from few tens of milliseconds to few days, but the latest data may definitely not be available within the fraction of millisecond.

- The schema may evolve over time as the application allows integration with other applications.

- Since the data can never be completely normalized or denormalized, the relationships *will* exist.

An example of this application is a web analytics application or a social microblogging platform. The key here is the scale of operation and staleness of data.

Another set of examples includes SaaS-based enterprise-grade applications such as CRM or ERP. One brilliant example of this is SalesForce—it is a SaaS application that allows you to integrate the data of your schema.

Entity schema requirements

For a web-scale application, general requirements on the entity schema include:

- Structured schema definition
- The ability to change schema over time without affecting existing records in any manner—in extreme case, latent schema
- Relationships may be optional at database layer and can be pushed to application layer mainly because of the low density

Data access requirements

From a data access perspective, we would have the following requirements:

- Partial record access
- Speed of operation execution — CRUD
- Inconsistent data — for a short moment — is tolerable

What NoSQL can do

For a web-scale application, NoSQL can help as follows:

- Everything already covered in the previous scenario.

  Document stores would be a fantastic choice for latent schema.

- It can provide scale of operations because it does not implement ACID operations but mostly provide BASE properties.

What NoSQL cannot do

I do not see any requirement that NoSQL cannot fulfill in this case. Note that we do not have ACID constraints — one of the main reasons why NoSQL was invented.

Decision

Use NoSQL. The choice of the type of store (data model) can vary depending upon the actual underlying requirement:

- In case of SaaS applications where the schema has to be flexible to incorporate user-specific attributes, document stores are the optimal choice. Examples of this subtype include applications such as CRM, ERP — mainly enterprise-targeted applications where each end consumer (organization) may have their own specific schema.
- In case of applications like e-learning or other social applications, whose underlying schema changes and evolves at a fast pace and would need the ability to change schema over time but still be under the tight control of the application developer, column-oriented database is a great choice.

- In the case of social applications that need ability to integrate with other application, it may want to use a mix of column-oriented and document-oriented store to mitigate the risk of complete schema overhaul of unforeseen data format of a new application that becomes a rage and this application must integrate with the new application in the market.

- To store relationships, graph databases may be an addendum to the actual data store. For example, Twitter uses graph database, **FlockDB** (`https://github.com/twitter/flockdb`), to store relationships while it uses Cassandra for real-time analytics (`http://www.slideshare.net/kevinweil/rainbird-realtime-analytics-at-twitter-strata-2011`), and most likely HBase for persistent store.

 Note that for Twitter, the latency requirement is less than 100 ms, as given in the presentation.

Summary

In this chapter, we did a comparative analysis of RDBMS versus NoSQL and the various models available in our quest to figure out what is the most suitable option, given a specific scenario.

Note however that these scenarios are only representational. In the application that you may be working on, you may still have to apply more brains to come up with the final solution. It is also possible that the final solution is a composite choice; one part data being in RDBMS while the other being in NoSQL store.

In the next chapter, we will compare the various databases and solutions available in the market. So, assuming that you plan to go ahead with at least some part of the data in a NoSQL store, the next chapter is a must read for you.

5

Comparative Study of NoSQL Products

Thus far we have looked at NoSQL from a purely technical perspective, comparing it with RDBMS as a technology choice. We also dug deep into understanding the various data models available while working with NoSQL.

In this chapter, we will do a comparative study of the various products available in the market for implementing NoSQL—both open source as well as commercial.

Specifically, we compare the following products:

- Amazon SimpleDB: `http://aws.amazon.com/simpledb`
- BaseX: `http://www.basex.org`
- Cassandra: `http://cassandra.apache.org`
- CouchDB: `http://couchdb.apache.org`
- Google Datastore: `http://developers.google.com/appengine`
- HBase: `http://hbase.apache.org`
- MemcacheDB: `http://memcachedb.org`
- MongoDB: `http://www.mongodb.com`
- Neo4j: `http://www.neo4j.org`
- Redis: `http://redis.io`

This chapter is structured such that we first explore each point for comparison and then compare it across the products.

Comparison

Choosing a technology does not merely involve a technical comparison. Several other factors related to documentation, maintainability, stability and maturity, vendor support, developer community, license, price, and the future of the product or the organization behind it also play important roles. Having said that, I must also add that technical comparison should continue to play a pivotal role.

We will start a deep technical comparison of the previously mentioned products and then look at the semi-technical and non-technical aspects for the same.

Technical comparison

From a technical perspective, we compare on the following parameters:

- Implementation language
- Engine types
- Speed

Implementation language

One of the more important factors that come into play is how can, if required, the product be extended; the programming language in which the product itself is written determines a large part of it. Some of the database may provide a different language for writing plugins but it may not always be true:

- **Amazon SimpleDB**: It is available in cloud and has a client SDK for Java, .NET, PHP, and Ruby. There are libraries for Android and iOS as well.
- **BaseX**: Written in Java. To extend, one must code in Java.
- **Cassandra**: Everything in Java.
- **CouchDB**: Written in Erlang. To extend use Erlang.
- **Google Datastore**: It is available in cloud and has SDK for Java, Python, and Go.
- **HBase**: It is Java all the way.
- **MemcacheDB**: Written in C. Uses the same language to extend.
- **MongoDB**: Written in C++. Client drivers are available in several languages including but not limited to JavaScript, Java, PHP, Python, and Ruby.
- **Neo4j**: Like several others, it is Java all the way.
- **Redis**: Written in C. So you can extend using C.

Great, so the first parameter itself may have helped you shortlist the products that you may be interested to use based on the developers available in your team or for hire. You may still be tempted to get smart people onboard and then build competency based on the choice that you make, based on subsequent dimensions.

Note that for the databases written in high-level languages like Java, it may still be possible to write extensions in languages like C or C++ by using interfaces like JNI or otherwise.

Amazon SimpleDB provides access via the HTTP protocol and has SDK in multiple languages. If you do not find an SDK for yourself, say for example, in JavaScript for use with NodeJS, just write one.

However, life is not open with Google Datastore that allows access only via its cloud platform App Engine and has SDKs only in Java, Python, and the Go languages. Since the access is provided natively from the cloud servers, you cannot do much about it. In fact, the top requested feature of the Google App Engine is support for PHP (See `http://code.google.com/p/googleappengine/issues/list`).

Engine types

Engine types define how you will structure the data and what data design expertise your team will need. As we discussed in *Chapter 4, Advantages and Drawbacks* NoSQL provides multiple options to choose from.

Database	Column oriented	Document store	Key value store	Graph
Amazon SimpleDB	No	No	Yes	No
BaseX	No	Yes	No	No
Cassandra	Yes	Yes	No	No
CouchDB	No	Yes	No	No
Google Datastore	Yes	No	No	No
HBase	Yes	No	No	No
MemcacheDB	No	No	Yes	No
MongoDB	No	Yes	No	No
Neo4j	No	No	No	Yes
Redis	No	Yes	Yes	No

You may notice two aspects of this table – a lot of No and multiple Yes against some databases. I expect the table to be populated with a lot more Yes over the next couple of years. Specifically, I expect the open source databases written in Java to be developed and enhanced actively providing multiple options to the developers.

Speed

One of the primary reasons for choosing a NoSQL solution is speed. Comparing and benchmarking the databases is a non-trivial task considering that each database has its own set of hardware and other configuration requirements.

Having said that, you can definitely find a whole gambit of benchmark results comparing one NoSQL database against the other with details of how the tests were executed.

Of all that is available, my personal choice is the **Yahoo! Cloud Serving Benchmark (YCSB)** tool. It is open source and available on Github at `https://github.com/brianfrankcooper/YCSB`. It is written in Java and clients are available for Cassandra, DynamoDB, HBase, HyperTable, MongoDB, Redis apart from several others that we have not discuss in this book.

Before showing some results from the YCSB, I did a quick run on a couple of easy-to-set-up databases myself. I executed them without any optimizations to just get a feel of how easy it is for software to incorporate it without needing any expert help.

I ran it on MongoDB on my personal box (server as well as the client on the same machine), DynamoDB connecting from a High-CPU Medium (c1.medium) box, and MySQL on the same High-CPU Medium box with both server and client on the same machine. Detailed configurations with the results are shown as follows:

Server configuration:

Parameter	MongoDB	DynamoDB	MySQL
Processor	5 EC2 Compute Units	N/A	5 EC2 Compute Units
RAM	1.7 GB with Apache HTTP server running (effective free: 200 MB, after database is up and running)	N/A	1.7GB with Apache HTTP server running (effective free: 500MB, after database is up and running)
Hard disk	Non-SSD	N/A	Non-SSD
Network configuration	N/A	US-East-1	N/A
Operating system	Ubuntu 10.04, 64 bit	N/A	Ubuntu 10.04, 64 bit
Database version	1.2.2	N/A	5.1.41
Configuration	Default	Max write: 500, Max read: 500	Default

Client configuration:

Parameter	MongoDB	DynamoDB	MySQL
Processor	5 EC2 Compute Units	5 EC2 Compute Units	5 EC2 Compute Units
RAM	1.7GB with Apache HTTP server running (effective free: 200MB, after database is up and running)	1.7GB with Apache HTTP server running (effective free: 500MB, after database is up and running)	1.7GB with Apache HTTP server running (effective free: 500MB after database is up and running)
Hard disk	Non-SSD	Non-SSD	Non-SSD
Network configuration	Same Machine as server	US-East-1	Same Machine as server
Operating system	Ubuntu 10.04, 64 bit	Ubuntu 10.04, 64 bit	Ubuntu 10.04, 64 bit
Record count	1,000,000	1,000	1,000,000
Max connections	1	5	1
Operation count (workload a)	1,000,000	1,000	1,000,000
Operation count (workload f)	1,000,000	100,000	1,000,000

Results:

Workload	Parameter	MongoDB	DynamoDB	MySQL
Workload-a (load)	Total time	290 seconds	16 seconds	300 seconds
	Speed (operations/ second)	2363 to 4180 (approximately 3700) Bump at 1278	50 to 82 (operations/ second)	3135 to 3517 (approximately 3300)
	Insert latency	245 to 416 microseconds (approximately 260) Bump at 875 microseconds	12 to 19 milliseconds	275 to 300 microseconds (approximately 290)

Workload	Parameter	MongoDB	DynamoDB	MySQL
Workload-a (run)	Total time	428 seconds	17 seconds	240 seconds
	Speed	324 to 4653	42 to 78	3970 to 4212
	Update latency	272 to 2946 microseconds	13 to 23.7 microseconds	219 to 225.5 microseconds
	Read latency	112 to 5358 microseconds	12.4 to 22.48 microseconds	240.6 to 248.9 microseconds
Workload-f (load)	Total time	286 seconds	Did not execute	295 seconds
	Speed	3708 to 4200		3254 to 3529
	Insert latency	228 to 265 microseconds		275 to 299 microseconds
Workload-f (run)	Total time	412 seconds	Did not execute	1022 seconds
	Speed	192 to 4146		224 to 2096
	Update latency	219 to 336 microseconds		216 to 233 microseconds, with two bursts at 600 and 2303 microseconds
	Read latency	119 to 5701 microseconds		1360 to 8246 microseconds
	Read Modify Write (RMW) latency	346 to 9170 microseconds		1417 to 14648 microseconds

Do not read too much into these numbers as they are a result of the default configuration, out-of-the-box setup without any optimizations.

Some of the results from YCSB published by Brian F. Cooper (http://www.brianfrankcooper.net/pubs/ycsb-v4.pdf) are shown next.

For update-heavy, 50-50 read-update:

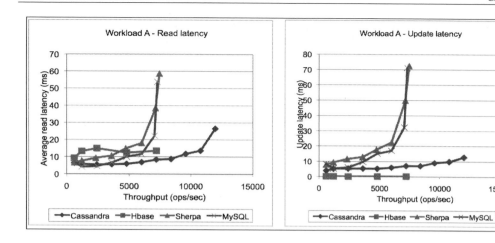

For read-heavy, under varying hardware:

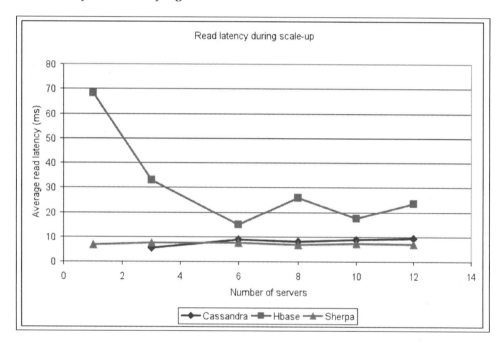

There are some more from Sergey Sverchkov at Altoros (`http://altoros.com/nosql-research`) who published their white paper recently.

For update-heavy, 50-50 read-update:

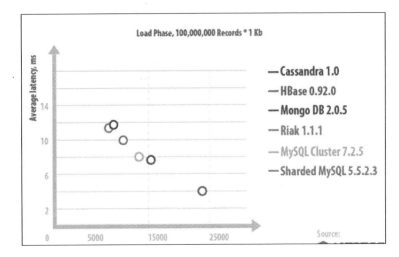

For read-heavy, 95-5 read-update:

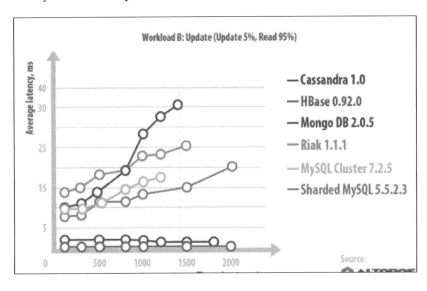

To conclude, there is no perfect NoSQL solution. As you will notice from the results, each database has its own profile and works amazingly under a set of conditions but may give horrendous results in other scenarios. A database that works awesomely in a read-heavy scenario may not be an optimal choice in an application that is write-heavy. Similarly, hardware configurations may affect some databases while others may operate independently allowing linear scaling out.

There are some more results from `http://www.cubrid.org/blog/dev-platform/nosql-benchmarking/`, comparing MongoDB, Cassandra, and HBase—just in case you are interested in exploring some more.

Features

Next we will compare the databases on the basis of various features like query language, support for bulk operations, record-size limits, limits on indexes, and anything related.

Limits

Most of the databases have limits on one or the other parameters that we will explore next.

- **Amazon SimpleDB**: Earlier it had a limit of 1000 bytes per value. As of today, unknown—most likely limited to few MBs. It can hold up to 10 GB or 1 billion records per domain. See this old but relevant discussion `http://bit.ly/SWuj8y` at stackoverflow.

- **BaseX**: BaseX stores complete XML documents, has a massive limit of 512GB, and allows for storage of a maximum of 229 files. An amazing illustration of the largest files created by its users—including Twitter, Wikipedia, MedLine—is available at `http://docs.basex.org/wiki/Statistics`. The largest file stored is about 420 GB. This limit is only per database instance. You can always cluster and increase your limits (except single file size).

- **Cassandra**: All data for one row must fit in one physical disk. Each column value should not be larger than 2 GB (231 bytes). Maximum number of columns per row is 2 billion (2 x 109), implying that each record may be no larger than 262 bytes. The column name has an additional limit of 64 KB. See the official documentation on limitations at `http://wiki.apache.org/cassandra/CassandraLimitations`. Note that versions prior to 0.7 had smaller limitations.

- **CouchDB**: Interestingly, the official document at `http://wiki.apache.org/couchdb/Frequently_asked_questions#How_Much_Stuff_can_I_Store_in_CouchDB.3F` says that the practical limits are unknown (read: never hit till date). Another discussion at `http://stackoverflow.com/questions/11019360/couchdb-document-size-limits` points that the configuration puts a limit of 4 GB, but again that may only be a default limit.

- **Google Datastore**: Maximum entity (row) size is only 1 MB while maximum transaction size is 10 MB. For a given entity, the maximum number of indexes is 20,000 and the maximum number of bytes in any index allowed is 2 MB. See official documentation at `https://developers.google.com/appengine/docs/python/datastore/overview#Quotas_and_Limits`.

- **HBase**: Per-record value must fit in the physical disk. However, cell value size is limited to 20 MB.

- **MemcacheDB**: Maximum object size is 1 MB.

- **MongoDB**: Maximum document size is 16 MB. Well, use GridFS API to store larger documents—practically unlimited size. Any composite/compound index may not have more than 31 fields while a single collection cannot have more than 64 indexes and each index cannot be larger than 1 KB. See `http://docs.mongodb.org/manual/reference/limits/` for all details.

- **Neo4j**: Documentation says that theoretically there are no limits. The default limit values are imposed only because of the typically available hardware. See `http://docs.neo4j.org/chunked/stable/capabilities-capacity.html#capabilities-data-size` for details.

- **Redis**: String value is limited to 512 MB while the upper limit on the size of the value for a key in general is 2 GB. Read `http://redis.io/topics/data-types` for details.

Bulk operations

By bulk operations, I refer to operations that involve multiple entities in a single go. In a typical SQL-based system, I can execute `DELETE FROM my_table where _id=1 or _id=2` allowing the deletion of multiple records at one go. Similarly for read, insert, and update operations.

Bulk read

It is interesting to note that not all databases support bulk reading of the records, that is a counterpart of the SQL statement `SELECT col1 FROM my_table where col2='val2'` may not exist for all NoSQL databases.

Document-oriented databases typically will support retrieval by a single record ID; and so will key-value stores. Column-oriented databases will, in general, allow multi-record read through one query.

Database	Supported	Example

SimpleDB	Yes	`https://sdb.amazonaws.com/`
		`?Action=Select`
		`&SelectExpression=select%20col1%20from%20`
		`my_table%20where %20col2%20%2D%20%27val2%27`

BaseX	Yes	`for $doc in collection()`
		`where value-of($doc//col2) = 'val2'`
		`return $doc//col1`

Cassandra	Yes	`select col1 from my_table` `where col2='val2'`

CouchDB	Yes	`function map(doc) {`
		`    if(doc.col2 == 'val2') {`
		`      emit(doc._id, doc.col1);`
		`    }`
		`}`
		`function reduce(k, v, rr) {`
		`  return v;`
		`}`

Datastore	Yes	`q = new Query('my_table').setFilter(`
		`    new FilterPredicate('col2',`
		`        FilerOperator.EQUAL, 'val2'));`
		`datastoreSvc.prepare(q).asIterable();`

HBase	Yes	`scan = new Scan().addColumn("col2".`
		`getBytes(), "val2".getBytes());`
		`results = htable.getScanner(scan);`

MemcacheDB	No	N/A
MongoDB	Yes	`db.my_table.find({ 'col2': 'val2' }, {` `'col1': 1 });`
Neo4j	No	Use Batch REST API. See `http://docs.neo4j.org/` `chunked/snapshot/rest-api-batch-ops.html`.
Redis	No	N/A

Bulk insert

By bulk insert I mean inserting multiple records using one command. The SQL counterpart of the same is shown as follows:

```
INSERT INTO my_table(_id, col1, col2) VALUES('_id1', 'v1', 1), ('_
id2', 'v2', 2)
```

It is very unlikely that databases that have only a HTTP-RESTful interface will support this since the record ID is part of the URL and document is part of the POST-body and multi-parts are not supported, at least not today. Having said that, it may still be supported in some more interesting ways, for example look at the SimpleDB option.

Database	Supported	Example

SimpleDB	Yes
	
	(Max 25 items, 256 attributes)
		`https://sdb.amazonaws.com/`
		`?Action=BatchPutAttributes`
		`&Item.1.ItemName=_id1`
		`&Item.1.Attribute.1.Name=col1`
		`&Item.1.Attribute.1.Value=v1`

BaseX	Yes	N/A. Could not find any reference to multiple documents at `http://docs.basex.org/wiki/Commands#ADD`.
Cassandra	Yes	CQL is very similar to SQL. Use standard SQL `INSERT` command syntax. See `http://cassandra.apache.org/doc/cql/CQL.html#INSERT`.

CouchDB	Yes	`curl -d '{"docs":[{"key":"baz","name":"bazz`
		`el"},`
		`   {"key":"bar","name":"barry"}]}'`
		`-X POST`
		`http://127.0.0.1:5984/my_db/_bulk_docs`

Datastore	Yes	`List<Entity> entities = ...` `datastoreSvc.put(entities);`
HBase	Yes	Since HBase follows MapReduce, the solution comprises of a lot of code. See `http://archive.cloudera.com/cdh/3/hbase/bulk-loads.html`.
MemcacheDB	No	N/A
MongoDB	Yes	`db.my_table.insert ([  { "_id": "doc1" },` `   { "_id": "doc2" }]);`
Neo4j	Yes	Use Batch REST API. See `http://docs.neo4j.org/chunked/snapshot/rest-api-batch-ops.html`.
Redis	No	N/A

Bulk update

Bulk update refers to the feature wherein multiple records may be updated using a single operation. Using SQL, we will execute:

```
UPDATE my_table SET(col1='new_value') WHERE col2 >= 3
```

Note that UPDATE is quite different from INSERT even though both change the state of the store. The UPDATE operation requires a record to exist. Even though a database may not support bulk insert, it is likely that it still may support bulk updates.

Database	Supported	Example
SimpleDB	Yes	`https://sdb.amazonaws.com/`
	(Max 25 items, 256 attributes)	`?Action=BatchPutAttributes`
		`&Item.1.ItemName=_id1`
		`&Item.1.Attribute.1.Name=col1`
		`&Item.1.Attribute.1.Value=v1`
BaseX	Yes	Use XQUF to update multiple documents at one go. `http://docs.basex.org/wiki/Update`.
Cassandra	Yes	CQL is very similar to SQL. Use the standard SQL UPDATE command syntax. See `http://cassandra.apache.org/doc/cql/CQL.html#UPDATE`.
CouchDB	Yes	Use Bulk Document API to first fetch required and then update them, or Update Handlers if the IDs are known. See `http://stackoverflow.com/a/8011725/332210`.
Datastore	Yes	`List<Entity> entities = ...`
		`datastoreSvc.put(entities);`
HBase	Yes	`HTableInterface ht = ...`
		`List<Put> items = ...`
		`ht.put(items);`
MemcacheDB	No	N/A
MongoDB	No	`db.collection.update({ 'col2': {$gte: 3 } },` `{ $set: { 'col1': 'new value' } }, false, true);`
Neo4j	Yes	Use Batch REST API. See `http://docs.neo4j.org/chunked/snapshot/rest-api-batch-ops.html`.
Redis	No	N/A

Bulk delete

Similar to the other bulk operations, the question is whether or not it is possible to delete multiple documents by issuing a single command. In SQL world, we execute the following statement:

```
DELETE FROM my_table WHERE _id='_id1'
```

Most of the NoSQL databases do support bulk delete operations.

Database	Supported	Example
SimpleDB	Yes	`https://sdb.amazonaws.com/` `?Action=BatchDeleteAttributes` `&Item.1.ItemName=_id1`
BaseX	Yes	`<delete path='xml-doc-prefix' />`
Cassandra	Yes	CQL can be used to delete not only rows but also columns from multiple rows. `DELETE col1 FROM my_table WHERE _id='id1'` to delete specific column. `DELETE FROM my_table WHERE id='_id1'` to delete the entire row.
CouchDB	Yes	As `http://bit.ly/SUtPP8` points, a deleted document has attribute `"_deleted": true`. You can use batch update to batch delete documents. See also `http://bit.ly/VSUXBb`.
Datastore	Yes (Keys only)	`List<Key> keys = ...` `datastoreSvc.delete(keys);`
HBase	Yes	`HTableInterface ht = ...` `List<Delete> items = ...` `ht.delete(items);`
MemcacheDB	No	N/A
MongoDB	Yes	`db.my_table.remove({ '_id': 'id1' });`
Neo4j	No	Use Batch REST API. See `http://docs.neo4j.org/chunked/snapshot/rest-api-batch-ops.html`.
Redis	Yes (Keys only)	`DEL key1 key2` `HDEL key1 key2`

Query options

What is a database if we cannot search it without having to know the primary key or the record ID. If you are just moving out from the RDBMS databases, you will be very much used to:

- Defining custom indexes for faster searches
- Searching across tables to create the final result using JOIN
- Creating complex views that will act as pseudo tables that can be queried upon

Get by ID

All databases support it. No questions asked.

Composite indexes

Now, this is a tricky requirement. Most of these databases allow searching across multiple attributes or columns or properties. Whether or not they allow defining custom composite index is a different question altogether.

Here, we are talking about searching within a table or model type. Note that since each database has its own terminology for defining the model structure, I will refer to it as model type (the tables in SQL world, entity for Datastore, and so on).

Database	Query with filters	Custom index
SimpleDB	Yes	No
BaseX	Yes	No
Cassandra	Yes	Yes
CouchDB	Yes	No
Datastore	Yes	Yes
HBase	Yes	Yes
MemcacheDB	No	No
MongoDB	Yes	Yes
Neo4j	Yes	Yes
Redis	No	No

Datastore does not allow non-equality comparison on more than one property.

If you look at the preceding table, you will notice that the key value stores, specifically, do not support filter queries.

Datastore mandates you to define a custom index before you can use it. Single-property queries are always supported unless the property is marked non-indexed, however, a query spanning multiple properties requires an explicit index to be created.

For document-oriented databases, multi-property queries are always supported irrespective of whether or not custom index definitions are allowed or required. MongoDB requires custom index definition for faster access whereas CouchDB always indexes it for you.

Cassandra uses the notion of what are known as secondary indexes for filter queries, while HBase supports using Hypertable (`HTableInterface`).

Views

Great, now that we know which database supports query by properties other than the key and support creating custom indexes before querying them, it is now time to look at if and how the different databases support querying across multiple model types.

While working with RDBMS/SQL, we use `JOIN` statements to create queries spanning across multiple tables.

The following is a table lists all possibilities.

Database	Cross-type query	Custom view definition
SimpleDB	Yes	No
BaseX	Yes	No
Cassandra	Yes	No
CouchDB	Yes	Yes
Datastore	No	No
HBase	Yes	No
MemcacheDB	No	No
MongoDB	Yes	No
Neo4j	Yes	No

Databases that do not support query filters can definitely not support cross-type queries since that requires non-ID field-based queries.

Among others, Datastore specifically does not support cross-type queries which means you cannot do things that you were so used to while working with RDBMS/SQL.

Document-oriented databases that are agnostic of the underlying document schema are the ones that do and will support cross-type queries, mainly because as far as the underlying database is concerned, it does not have any notion of type or schema. Each piece of content is—simply put—a semi-structured document that can be indexed and searched.

CouchDB is the only database in our list that supports creating custom view definition that persists as well. Note that other document-oriented databases support indexing—either implicit or explicit—but do not support creating named views that can be queried upon. Additionally, these views do not compare to RDBMS views. CouchDB views do not have any schema prescribed and are a result of the reduce-step in the operation. As such, the performance benefit is not comparable to as in RDBMS views. More details on CouchDB views are available at `http://wiki.apache.org/couchdb/HTTP_view_API`.

Security

The next aspect that we compare is security. Well, no database has been implemented without keeping security in mind but then each database defines various aspects of security in its own way.

Access management

Under access management, we compare the following:

- Authentication
- Authorization

Authentication

Well, a basic requirement for any database server is authentication and authorized access. Let's look at what access mechanisms are available with each database:

Database	Authentication support
SimpleDB	Each request requires a access key and HMAC-based signature to validate the requests.
BaseX	Gives commands – `CREATE USER`, `ALTER USER`, `DROP USER`. It has a simple username- and password-based login.
Cassandra	Uses a username/password combo. Passwords can, optionally, be MD5-hashed. But always kept in a text file.

Database	Authentication support
CouchDB	Provides RESTful access to manage users.
	Authentication can be either HTTP-Basic or Cookie-based.
	Since Version 0.11, OAuth authentication is supported.
	See `http://bit.ly/UhKHwc`.
Datastore	No authentication. Runs directly from Google App Engine.
HBase	Kerberos-based authentication is supported.
MemcacheDB	N/A
MongoDB	Username/password combo. Admin is a special user.
	The REST API for admin must be either disabled or firewalled as it does not provide any security.
Neo4j	Provides an API-based highly flexible authentication support. Allows you to write custom logic.
Redis	N/A

Authorization or role-based access

Role-based access allows you to configure what permissions each account or group of accounts is granted. You do not want all users to always have administrative privileges. A comparison table enlisting options available with each database is shown next.

In general there can be the following permissions associated with an account:

- **None (N)** – akin to disabled account.
- **Read (R)** – can only read data, per database or collection.
- **Write (W)** – can read as well as write (includes insert, edit, and delete), per database or collection.
- **Create (C)** – can read, write, and also create table, per database or collection.
- **Database Admin (D)** – can administer a specific database or collection.
- **Server Admin (A)** – can RWC and also add database or collection, administer accounts and permissions. Can do everything possible with the server.

Database	Authorization support
SimpleDB	No. Each `AccessKey` that can be authenticated has all privileges.
BaseX	Can configure one or more of NRWCA permissions with any account. Can configure at database level.

Database	Authorization support
Cassandra	Can configure permissions at keyspace (akin to tables) or column-family level. Permissions are restricted to R/W.
CouchDB	Can configure permissions at database level. Permissions available – RDA. See `http://bit.ly/SOZ3Fj`.
Datastore	N/A
HBase	Supports configuring access control lists. Permissions available – RWCA. See `http://bit.ly/TDwRGf` and `http://bit.ly/RO28b3`.
MemcacheDB	N/A
MongoDB	Permissions available at server level. No collection-level permissions available. Permissions available are RA.
Neo4j	API-based authorization gives you complete control over what you wan—can be as fine-grained or coarse-grained as you need. See `http://bit.ly/RO2uyj`.
Redis	N/A

Encryption

Access control is only one form of security that one would require. In real enterprises, there is a definitive need for stronger security. Specifically, one may want encryption support. Data stored and/or data transferred may need to be encrypted while synchronizing across data centers.

Database	Store encryption	Protocol encryption
SimpleDB	No	No
BaseX	No	No
Cassandra	No	Yes
		Internode access uses TLS/SSL
CouchDB	No	Yes
		(`http://bit.ly/POrAx6` and `http://bit.ly/TACUcl`)
Datastore	No	No
HBase	No	No
		(`http://bit.ly/VVmxOO`)
MemcacheDB	No	No
MongoDB	Yes	Yes
		(`http://bit.ly/RO40R1`)

Database	Store encryption	Protocol encryption
Neo4j	Yes (http://bit.ly/XwvX3m)	Yes
Redis	No	No

Third-party tools like zNcrypt support store-level encryption. See list of supported applications at http://www.gazzang.com/support/supported-applications.

 I do not personally endorse this product. Do evaluate before you use it.

Multitenancy

Multitenancy allows you to scale your database to classify and segregate data across multiple applications or organizations without having a need for a separate installation.

According to Wikipedia:

> *Multitenancy refers to a principle in software architecture where a single instance of the software runs on a server, serving multiple client organizations (tenants).*

The question is, at database level, what does multitenancy really mean? There are two ways that your application using one of these databases can be multitenant:

- The application is multitenant irrespective of the underlying database. It is so by the way underlying model and entities are defined. For example, portal servers like SharePoint and Liferay are multitenant within a single database.

- The entities are not modeled keeping multitenancy deployment, for example in case of legacy applications wherein you may just want to rewrite the data-access layer rather than the data-processing (business logic) layer. In this case, you want support for multiple databases or collections within one server installation.

When I say multitenant database, I refer to the second option.

Database	Multitenancy support
SimpleDB	No
BaseX	Yes
Cassandra	Yes

Database	Multitenancy support
CouchDB	Yes
Datastore	No
HBase	No
MemcacheDB	No
MongoDB	Yes
Neo4j	Yes
Redis	No

SimpleDB and Datastore are multitenant by very nature of cloud deployment. However, within one instance, there is no further subclassification. So, you cannot use the second approach, mentioned previously, to make your application multitenant. In fact, it will not even be required for database to support it.

RDBMS related features

One of the more common queries that I have seen people having is support for counterparts for the RDBMS features, specifically support for JOIN, VIEW, and transactions (ACID).

Well, as we discussed in previous chapters, that is not really what NoSQL has been invented for. But nevertheless, the vendors and community have striven to provide some of these in as much capacity as possible.

We have already discussed about JOIN (cross-type queries) and VIEW earlier.

As far as transaction support is concerned, I have not read or heard any database writing or talking about it except for Neo4j. See http://bit.ly/TAHcAs for the official documentation of Neo4j on transaction support.

Deployment and maintenance

Let us shift our focus from core development to service engineering and explore the parameters of support and features under availability, automatic failover, replication, backup, restore, recovery from crash, and so on.

Availability

A database is a shared resource used by a cluster of application servers. As such, it becomes highly desirable that it supports clustering, load balancing, and automatic failover.

The table listing what is available with which database is shown as follows:

Database	Clustering	Load balancing	Automatic failover
SimpleDB	N/A	N/A	N/A
BaseX	NO [1]	No	No
Cassandra	Yes [2]	Yes [3]	Yes [4]
CouchDB	No [5]	Yes [6]	Yes
Datastore	N/A	N/A	N/A
HBase	Yes [7]	Yes [8,9]	Yes
MemcacheDB	Yes [10]	No	No [11]
MongoDB	Yes [12]	Yes [13]	Yes [14]
Neo4j	Yes [15]	Yes [16]	Yes
Redis	No [17]	NO	No

For cloud-hosted databases, such as SimpleDB and Datastore, we are not much concerned about the internal service engineering aspects as long as the database is available from the application.

References used in the preceding table are as follows:

- [1] http://www.mail-archive.com/basex-talk@mailman.uni-konstanz.de/msg01477.html
- [2] http://www.datastax.com/docs/0.8/cluster_architecture/cluster_planning
- [3] http://wiki.apache.org/cassandra/Operations#Load_balancing
- [4] http://prettyprint.me/2010/03/03/load-balancing-and-improved-failover-in-hector/
- [5] http://guide.couchdb.org/draft/clustering.html
- [6] http://guide.couchdb.org/draft/balancing.html
- [7] http://hbase.apache.org/replication.html
- [8] http://hbase.apache.org/book/architecture.html#arch.overview.nosql
- [9] http://hstack.org/why-were-using-hbase-part-1/
- [10] http://osdir.com/ml/memcachedb/2009-03/msg00027.html
- [11] http://www.couchbase.com/forums/thread/load-balance-memcached
- [12] http://docs.mongodb.org/manual/core/sharding/
- [13] http://stackoverflow.com/questions/5500441/mongodb-load-balancing

- [14] http://www.mongodb.org/display/DOCS/Replica+Sets
- [15] http://docs.neo4j.org/chunked/stable/ha-setup-tutorial.html
- [16] http://docs.neo4j.org/chunked/stable/ha-haproxy.html
- [17] http://redis.io/topics/cluster-spec

Maintenance

Next in line are the backup options – full and incremental, and database import/export options.

Database	Full backup	Incremental backup	Import/export
SimpleDB	N/A	N/A	N/A
BaseX	Yes [1]	No	No
Cassandra	Yes [2]	Yes [2]	Yes [3]
CouchDB	Yes [4]	Yes [5]	No[6]
Datastore	N/A	N/A	N/A
HBase	Yes [7]	Yes [8]	Yes [9]
MemcacheDB	Yes [10]	No	No
MongoDB	Yes [11]	No[12]	Yes [13]
Neo4j	Yes [14]	Yes [14]	No
Redis	Yes [15, 16]	No	No

The table has been compiled using the following references:

- [1] http://docs.basex.org/wiki/Commands#CREATE_BACKUP
- [2] http://www.datastax.com/docs/1.0/operations/backup_restore
- [3] http://wiki.apache.org/cassandra/Operations#Import_.2BAC8_export
- [4] http://wiki.apache.org/couchdb/How_to_make_filesystem_backups
- [5] http://comments.gmane.org/gmane.comp.db.couchdb.user/11410
- [6] http://www.rossbates.com/2009/07/data-migration-for-couchdb/
- [7] http://hbase.apache.org/book/ops.backup.html
- [8] http://www.slideshare.net/neallee/hbase-incremental-backup
- [9] http://hbase.apache.org/book/ops_mgt.html#export
- [10] http://www.docunext.com/wiki/MemcacheDB#Backing_Up_MemcacheDB_Data

- [11] http://www.mongodb.org/display/DOCS/Backups
- [12] http://www.mongodb.org/display/DOCS/Backups#Backups-IncrementalBackups
- [13] http://docs.mongodb.org/manual/administration/import-export/
- [14] http://docs.neo4j.org/chunked/stable/operations-backup.html
- [15] http://redis.io/topics/persistence
- [16] http://redis4you.com/articles.php?id=010&name=Redis+save+and+backup+script

Tools

Working with API and libraries is great, but how about some easy to use, quick to start tools? It does not matter if the tool is an official tool from the team or a third-party tool, as long as one exists, I have documented it.

The following table summarizes the support for various kinds of tools – **Command Line Interface (CLI)** aka shell, GUI tools, and web-based management.

Database	CLI	Desktop GUI			Web
		Windows	**Mac**	**Linux**	
SimpleDB	Yes [1]	Yes [25]	Yes [25]	Yes [25]	N/A
BaseX	Yes [2]	Yes [3]	Yes [3]	Yes [3]	No
Cassandra	Yes [4, 8]	Yes [5]	Yes [5]	Yes [5]	Yes [6, 7]
CouchDB	Yes [9] (CURL)	Yes [9, 10]	Yes [9]	Yes [9]	Yes [9] (CURL)
Datastore	No	No	No	No	No
HBase	Yes [11]	Yes [12]	Yes [12]	Yes [12]	Yes [13] (Built-in)
MemcacheDB	Yes [14]	No	No	No	No
MongoDB	Yes [15]	Yes [16, 18]	Yes [16, 17]	Yes [16]	Yes [19]
Neo4j	Yes [20]	No	No	No	Yes [21]
Redis	Yes [22]	Yes [23]	Yes [23]	Yes [23]	Yes [24]

References:

- [1] http://code.google.com/p/amazon-simpledb-cli/
- [2] http://docs.basex.org/wiki/Standalone_Mode

- [3] http://docs.basex.org/wiki/Graphical_User_Interface
- [4] http://wiki.apache.org/cassandra/CassandraCli
- [5] http://code.google.com/a/apache-extras.org/p/cassandra-gui/
- [6] http://wiki.apache.org/cassandra/Administration%20Tools
- [7] https://github.com/hmsonline/virgil
- [8] http://wiki.apache.org/cassandra/NodeTool
- [9] http://wiki.apache.org/couchdb/Related_Projects
- [10] http://kanapeside.com/
- [11] http://wiki.apache.org/hadoop/Hbase/Shell
- [12] http://sourceforge.net/projects/hbasemanagergui/
- [13] http://hbaseexplorer.wordpress.com/hbaseexplorer/
- [14] https://github.com/andrewgross/memcache-cli
- [15] http://www.mongodb.org/display/DOCS/mongo+-
  +The+Interactive+Shell
- [16] http://www.mongodb.org/display/DOCS/Admin+UIs
- [17] http://mongohub.todayclose.com/
- [18] http://www.mongovue.com/
- [19] http://www.mongodb.org/display/DOCS/Http+Interface
- [20] http://docs.neo4j.org/chunked/stable/shell.html
- [21] http://docs.neo4j.org/chunked/stable/tools-webadmin.html
- [22] http://redis.io/topics/quickstart
- [23] http://bit.ly/VW7owf
- [24] http://webd.is/
- [25] http://www.razorsql.com/features/simpledb_features.html

Protocol

The final technical bit that I will touch upon is transport protocol that is used for data transfer — between the server and the client. For the sake of simplicity, I will classify the protocols under the following heads:

- **HTTP**: Standard protocol. May or may not support RESTful interface, but that is fine. The message format is expected to be text (JSON or XML or otherwise).

- **TCP**: The TCP protocol that optimizes bandwidth consumption (binary) or otherwise (text). If it's binary, it is generally non-interoperable except using the provided drivers or tools.

- **Thrift**: Also known as the Apache Thrift protocol. It is an **Interface Definition Language (IDL)** to implement services that can be consumed from across the languages. Originally developed by Facebook, it is now maintained by the Apache Foundation. As per the Apache Thrift website:

  The Apache Thrift software framework, for scalable cross-language services development, combines a software stack with a code generation engine to build services that work efficiently and seamlessly between C++, Java, Python, PHP, Ruby, Erlang, Perl, Haskell, C#, Cocoa, JavaScript, Node.js, Smalltalk, OCaml and Delphi, and other languages.

Database	Protocol
SimpleDB	H
BaseX	TCP-Text
Cassandra	Thrift
CouchDB	HTTP
Datastore	N/A
HBase	Thrift
MemcacheDB	TCP-Binary
MongoDB	TCP-Binary
Neo4j	Multiple
Redis	TCP-Binary

Nontechnical comparison

Let us shift gears a bit and look at some nontechnical parameters to compare the databases.

Source and license

License plays a critical role in taking a final business decision on choosing a database. While commercial license—with or without source code—had been the norm especially in the enterprise application where the main drivers were vendor support and protection of intellectual property, things have started to change in recent times.

Because of strong vendor and community support, companies have started to adopt open source libraries and applications. Given comparable metrics on other parameters, the final decision boils down to the license.

Distributable applications prefer Apache, BSD, MIT, X11, and other compatible licenses while in-the-cloud applications also use GPL-licensed code. AGPL is a license to fret unless there is dual licensing available for commercial license to protect intellectual properties.

Database	Commercial	OSS Commercial	OSS Open	License
SimpleDB	N/A	N/A	N/A	N/A
BaseX	N/A	Yes	No	BSD
Cassandra	N/A	Yes	No	
CouchDB	No	Yes	No	
Datastore	N/A	N/A	N/A	N/A
HBase	No	Yes	No	
MemcacheDB	No	Yes	No	BSD-like
MongoDB	Yes	No	Yes	G
Neo4j	Yes	No	Yes	GPL, G
Redis	N/A	Yes	No	BSD

In SimpleDB and Datastore, neither the source code nor the binaries are available, hence the concept of license, as we are evaluating, is not applicable.

OSS Commercial refers to the licenses that allow you to develop commercial applications while protecting your intellectual property by not forcing you to contribute the code back to the community, while OSS Open refers to the license that asks you to contribute the code back to the community to ensure that everyone benefits at large (like the way you did by forking the code from the community).

The last column shows the actual license under which the code is available.

In the databases that we have covered in this chapter, three of them—Cassandra, CouchDB, and HBase—are maintained by the Apache Foundation and use one of the most liberal open source licenses – Apache License v2.

Source code of MongoDB is available under dual licenses – AGPL and commercial. Should you wish to use MongoDB in your applications, distributed or otherwise, do not forget to buy a commercial license.

Community and vendor support

Last but not least, we compare these databases on the key parameter of support availability. This can be further subclassified into two parts:

- **Community**: A strong community means a lot. It shows that a lot of people are using it, which in turn implies that it is a good option. It results in faster response time to the queries, you no longer have to depend on the developers or a vendor to always respond.

- **Vendor support**: A vendor providing complete solution support means a lot to the company whose core competency is not technology. Imagine a travel or a finance company having to spend more time in trying to get around provisioning a database to suit their conditions rather than on implementing the actual business layer of the application.

I have classified community support into four broad categories:

- **Forums**: Open discussion forums and mailing lists which one can subscribe, ask questions, and get a response from the community.
- **Users**: Number of users discussing on the forum. I am interested in **Monthly Active Users (MAU)**.
- **Discussions**: Number of discussions on the forums.
- **StackOverflow**: Whether there is a tag for the databases or not, and if so, total number of questions tagged.

The sizing has been done as follows:

- **Small**
  - One, or at best, a couple of discussion forums
  - Activity from less than 100 users a month
  - Total discussions that are less than 300 per month
  - Total number of questions tagged and responded to that are less than 1,000

- **Medium**
  - Three discussion forums
  - Activity from over 100 but less than 1,000 users a month
  - Total discussions that are less than 3,000 per month
  - Total number of questions tagged and responded to that are less than 5,000

- **Large**
  - ○ A value bigger than that in large on any each parameter

Database	Forum	User	Discussion	StackOverflow		Vendor
				Tag	Size	
SimpleDB	S	S	S	Yes	S	Yes
BaseX	S	S	S	Yes	S	Yes
Cassandra	M	M	M	Yes	M	Yes
CouchDB	M	M	M	Yes	M	Yes
Datastore	S	M	M	Yes	M	Yes
HBase	M	M	M	Yes	M	Yes
MemcacheDB	Defunct	S	S	Yes	S	No
MongoDB	M	L	L	Yes	L	Yes
Neo4j	S	M	M	Yes	S	Yes
Redis	S	S	S	Yes	S	Yes

The Tag column indicates whether or not StackOverflow has a special category for this database.

Summary

In this chapter, we did a detailed comparative study of a subset of NoSQL databases available in the market on various parameters—both technical and nontechnical.

Note that this comparison holds good at the time of writing this book. As databases evolve and get contributions especially from the open source community, the comparison tables are bound to change.

As a result of the feature enhancements, expect an upsurge in the community size and more vendors to start providing solutions and support.

The next and the last chapter of the book will give you the run down of a case study showing how to effectively use and implement NoSQL in your application or organization.

6

Case Study

So, with all the text that you have read so far, do you feel confident enough to go ahead with implementing your next application using NoSQL?

If you have even the slightest of doubts, this chapter is for you.

In this chapter, we will run through a simple application, from the concept to the final implementation. We implement the application using MongoDB—a document store.

 There is no particular reason for choosing MongoDB except that it is easy to set up and quick to go. As such, we spend less time in exploring and setting up the database and rather focus and spend more time on the actual implementation.

The purpose of this walk-through is multifold:

- First, we look at how to attack the problem.
- Next, we look at—based on the database choice—what constraints we are working against.
- Then, we identify the tools that we need to have.
- Subsequently, we do the database design, the same old stuff of schema definition, normalization, denormalization. Be ready for some surprises here.
- Finally, we look at the actual code to implement it.

Application definition

People have been keeping a log of their daily activities for ages. With the advent of the internet, they got a new place to write and share. We call this Weblog or, simply, blog. A blog comprised of of posts, typically shown in reverse chronology.

For our case study, we will create a simple blog application that supports the following:

- Showing up latest posts, with support for pagination, in reverse chronology and a specific post.
- Writing new posts, editing, and deleting the same.
  - Support for multiple authors in a blog
- Hierarchical categories. Map posts to a specific category.
- Flat, nonhierarchical tags. Map post to multiple tags.
- Support for comments on individual posts.
- Support for custom plugins that may have custom data requirements.

Requirement analysis

We can translate these user features into the following technical requirements as far as the database and schema is concerned:

- Multitenant, high scalable database
- More reads than writes to the databases
- Role-based access to the application—extensible model
- Extensible schema
- Support to store searchable text, computable numeric, and raw-binary data store
- Data access may require cross-entity access (aka JOIN)

Note that these technical requirements are only representational, they will help us focus on the database than the actual application.

Implementation using MongoDB

The first database that we use to implement the store for the application is MongoDB. The engine type is document store with JSON as the underlying structure.

Features and constraints

Given next are some of the features available with MongoDB:

- Document-oriented store with latent schema

- Uses the binary JSON (BSON) format

- Typed values – string, int, double, boolean, date, bytearray, object, array

- Support for multiple databases, known as collections

- Support for map-reduce (useful in batch processing and aggregations)

- Support for ad hoc queries using user-defined functions (in JavaScript)

- Master-slave replications, load-balancing using sharding

MongoDB has its own set of challenges. Some of them are given next (`http://blog.engineering.kiip.me/post/20988881092/a-year-with-mongodb`, `http://blog.iprofs.nl/2011/11/25/is-mongodb-a-good-alternative-to-rdbms-databases-like-oracle-and-mysql/`):

- Field name's storage is not optimized. It is advised to use short names. See `http://www.mongodb.org/display/DOCS/Optimizing+Storage+of+Small+Objects` for some guidelines.

- Indexes are memory heavy (`http://qr.ae/1QSdm`).

- Unreliable – if it crashes during an update, you lose all data (`http://qr.ae/1QSdm`).

- Map-reduce is not blazingly fast.

- Imposed limit of 24,000 namespaces (collections and indexes) per database (`http://blog.serverdensity.com/notes-from-a-production-mongodb-deployment/`).

Setup

Download MongoDB server from `http://www.mongodb.org/downloads`. Although there are Java drivers available, they are not very friendly as the queries still use the native BSON syntax. Let us use Mongoose, the official driver from 10gen. You can download it from `http://mongoosejs.com/docs/index.html`. It requires `Node.js` that can be downloaded from `http://nodejs.org/download`.

For the purpose of our case study, we will name the collection – blog. Note that in MongoDB, it is not required to create a collection before it is used.

Database design

One of the tenets of database modeling for NoSQL is that you design less based on the data entities and their relationships and more on the basis of queries that you would run against the database.

There are a few things that you will probably need to unlearn and forget; normalization, foreign keys, and JOIN.

One thing that you will need to learn, practice, and master is appropriate granularity of denormalization. Whenever in doubt, ask yourself a simple question, "What do I want to fetch?" and you will be very close to the denormalization granularity.

Database queries

Defining database queries is a critical step before modeling. You don"t have to know of the distant future but it"s always better to know as many queries as possible at the start of a development cycle.

At a high level, queries will be required for the following:

- Post-related queries:
    - Retrieve a list of all posts in reverse chronology or the latest N posts
    - Add or edit one post, with support for revision history
    - Delete one or more posts
    - Retrieve details of one post including categories, tags, and comments

- Category-related queries:
    - Retrieve all categories hierarchically
    - Add or edit a category
    - Delete one or more categories
    - Link or delink one or more posts against a category

- Tag-related queries:
    - Mostly same as for category except that the tags are not hierarchical
    - Link or delink one or more posts against one or more categories

I have deliberately omitted user- and role-related queries including CRUD operations for a user and associating roles for a user for brevity.

Along with the queries mentioned earlier, we need to support extensible schema requirements for new plugins that the application must support.

Database modeling

Now that we have a fair idea of our queries, it is time to define the database entities. It is important to note that though we may end up with data redundancy, the degree of denormalization granularity will not be single handedly driven by queries. The data model supported by the database also plays a key role.

Using the query requirements mentioned earlier, we can come up with the following basic entities to support core functionality:

- Post and PostRevision
- Comment
- Category
- Tag

PostRevision keeps track of versions of a post. One of these revisions is visible to the users.

We will look at supporting plugin-specific data in a while.

The following relationships exist for the entities:

- One-to-many between Post and Comment
- One-to-many between Post and PostRevision
- Many-to-one between Post and Category
- Many-to-many between Post and Category

With the relationships in mind for these entities, we get the structure as follows:

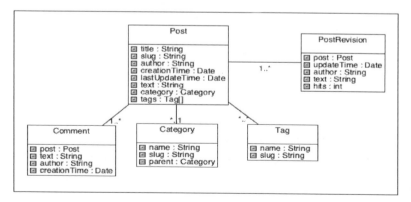

All entities are assumed to have a unique identifier. MongoDB uses the `_id` field for the unique identifier for the entity. It can either be provided or autogenerated. I prefer use an autogenerated identifier as opposed to that provided while working with MongoDB. See the discussion at `http://snmaynard.com/`.

Schema definition

With document-store we have great leverage over the entity schema. Although MongoDB supports latent schema, it makes a definite sense to start with a schema and update it over time as the need may be.

```
// Entity Tag
var entityTag = {
  name: String,
  slug: String
};
// Entity Category
var entityCategory = {
  name: String,
  slug: String,
  parent: { type: Schema.Types.ObjectId, ref: "Category" }
};
// Entity Comment
var entityComment = {
  author: String,
  text: String,
  creationTime: { type: Date, "default": Date.now },
  post: { type: Schema.Types.ObjectId, ref: "Post" }
};
```

The `Post` entity can be defined in one of the following two ways:

- Comprising only of references to `PostRevision` indicating which revision is the published revision
- Comprising of copy of content from `PostRevision`, duplicating the records

The former approach optimizes the storage space whereas the latter approach reduces the time to retrieve the published posts so that the load time of the pages is reduced. `PostRevision`, on the other hand, has a reference to the main `Post` against which the revisions are created.

I would take up the latter approach, sacrificing space in favor of speed. Based on this, the structure of `Post` and `PostRevision` is shown as follows, with the portion of the schema duplicating the post-related content highlighted:

```
// Entity Post
var entityPost = {
  title: String,
  slug: String,
  author: String,
  creationTime: { type: Date, "default": Date.now },
  lastUpdateTime: { type: Date, "default": Date.now },
  text: String,
  category: { type: Schema.Types.ObjectId,
              ref: "Category" },
  tags: [{ type: Schema.Types.ObjectId,
              ref: "Category" }]

};
// Entity PostRevision
var entityPostRevision = {
  updateTime: { type: Date, "default": Date.now },
  author: String,
  text: String,
  hits: int,
  post: { type: Schema.Types.ObjectId, ref: "Post" }
};
```

With these schema definitions, we now need to register them with Mongoose:

```
// Register schemas using Mongoose
var db = require("mongoose"),
    Schema = db.Schema;

var schemaTag = new Schema(entityTag),
    schemaCategory = new Schema(entityCategory),
    schemaComment = new Schema(entityComment),
    schemaPost = new Schema(entityPost),
    schemaPostRevision = new
                Schema(PentityostRevision);

var Tag = db.model(schemaTag),
    Category = db.model(schemaCategory),
    Comment = db.model(schemaComment),
    Post = db.model(schemaPost),
    PostRevision = db.model(schemaPostRevision);
```

Even though it looks complex, it actually gives you a lot of power. The driver is obtained and stored in the db variable. The model method of the driver registers the Schema and provides helper methods and properties (autogenerated). We will explore them as we go along with the case study.

Note that Mongoose will ensure a _id field that will be an autogenerated primary key, unless specified otherwise.

Writing queries

Let us analyze writing queries for the following scenarios:

- A simple query involving one entity. The result set may comprise one or more records.

- A query involving one entity with a subset of columns that may be used for aggregate results (for example, count, sum, average, and so on) or otherwise.

- A query across entities with one-to-one relationship.

- A query across entities with one-to-many relationship.

- A query across entities with many-to-many relationship.

Queries for a single entity, simple result

Let us look at the code for the CRUD operations on a Tag entity:

```
// Insert a new record
var t = new Tag({
  name: "NoSQL",
  slug: "nosql"
});
// Auto-generated method save, async call
t.save(function(err, tag) {
  if(err) {
    //handle rror
  }
});
// Update the tag
t.name = "No SQL";
t.save(function(err, tag) { });
// Retrieve by id
id = db.Types.ObjectId.fromString("abcdef0123456789abcdefab");
Tag.findById(id, function(err, tag) {

});
```

```
// Delete a tag
t = getTagToDelete();
t.remove(function(err, resp) { });
// Delete a tag, given its slug
var s = getSlugToRemove();
Tag.remove({ "slug": s }, function(err, resp) { });
```

Queries for a single entity, Aggregate

The query to get a count of all tags and to get count of all posts for a given tag is
as follows:

```
// Simple count, all tags
Tag.count(function(err, count) {
  console.log("Total number of tags: " + count);
});
// Count of posts for a given tag
var t = getTagToSearchFor();
Post.count({ tags: t },
  function(err, count) {
    console.log("Total posts for tag " + t.name
      + " is: " + count);
});
// Total hits for a post
Post.findOne({ "slug": "beginiing-nosql-database" },
  function(err, post) {
    if(!err && post) {
      PostRevision.find({ "post": post }).
        .select({ count: 1 })
        .function(e, postRevisions) {
          var totalHits = 0;
          if(!e && postRevisions) {
            postRevisions.forEach(function(p) {
              totalHits += (p.hits || 0);
            });
          }
        });
    }
});
```

Older versions of MongoDB do not perform well with the count command. It is advisable to not use this command frequently. The ticket on this issue—https://jira. mongodb.org/browse/SERVER-1752—is closed. The fix, however, will be available from v2.3.2, which is not a production release as of the writing of this book.

Queries for one-to-one relationship

Well, in our case study, we do not have any one-to-one relationship. While working with NoSQL, it is always advisable to merge the one-to-one relationship entities. Since most of the databases allow the adding of properties or columns on demand, extending schema is mostly trivial.

Queries for one-to-many relationship

In the blog application, one category may have multiple posts. Similarly, we can have multiple revisions and comments for a given post. At a high level, we have the following two scenarios in this category:

- **One-to-many**: All posts within a category, comments for a post, and all revisions for a post
- **Many-to-one perspective**: Category of a post, post associated with a particular comment, and main post for a revision

Note that we have a reference to Category in Post and of Post in PostRevision. We can use this to filter the Post or PostRevision data. The code will be as given next:

```
// Retrieve all posts for category with slug, say, "nosql"
Category.findOne({ "slug": "nosql"},
  function(err, category) {
    if(!err) {
      Post.find({ "category": category },
        function(e, posts) {
          for(var p in posts) {
            console.log("Post: " + p.title);
          }
      });
    }
});
// Retrieve category associated with a post
var id = getIdOfPost();
Post.findById(id, function(err, post) {
```

```
    if(!err) {
      var c = post.category;
      console.log(p.title + " belongs to " + c.title);
    }
  });
```

As you see, retrieval queries require two finds—one for the category and second for the actual post—in the first case. Reason is that the category information is not duplicated in the post records. So, we first get the category reference and then the list of posts in that particular category.

Can we do better? We will explore this question in the *Model refinements* section given later in the chapter.

Let us now see the queries required to update the details associated with category and posts. We will explore the following scenarios:

- Changing the category of a post
- Changing the details of a category for a given post
- Deleting all posts or posts within a date-range inside a category
- Deleting a category and moving all posts to a default category

```
// Move a post to a different category
var cat = getNewCategoryToMoveTo();

Post.findById("0123456789abcdef01234567",
  function(err, post) {
    if(!err) {
      post.category = cat;
      post.save(function(err, savedPost) { });
    }
  });
// Change the details of category associated with a post
var postSlug = getSlugOfPostToChange();

Post.findOne({ "slug": postSlug }).
  .populate("category")
  .exec(function(err, post) {
    if(!err) {
      var c = post.category;
      c.name = "NoSQL Databases";
      c.slug = "nosql-databases";
      c.save(function(e, cat) { });
    }
```

```
});
// Add a post and associate it with a new category
var catDatabases = getParentCategory();
var cat = new Category({
  name: "Non-Relational Database",
  slug: "non-relational-database"
  parent: catDatabases
});

cat.save(function(e, c) {
  if(!e) {
    var post = new Post({
      title: "What are non-relational datbases",
      slug: "what-are-non-relational-databases",
      text: "Main content of the post",
      category: c,
      author: "Gaurav Vaish",
      tags: [ tag1, tag2, tag3 ]
    });
    post.save(function(e, savedPost) { });
  }
});
// Delete all posts within a category
var catId = getCategoryId();
Category.findById(catId, function(err, category) {
  if(!err) {
    Post.remove({ "category": category },
      function(err, response) {
      });
  }
});
// Delete a category
//    and move all related posts to a default category
var oldCat = getCategoryToDelete();
var newCat = getDefaultCategory();

Post.find({ "category": oldCat }, function(e, posts) {
  posts.forEach(function(p) {
    p.category = newCat;
  });
  //Mongoose-hack. See http://bit.ly/13n6UCN
  oldCat.remove();
  Post.collection.insert(posts, function(e, r) { });
});
```

Queries for many-to-many relationship

Many-to-many relationship exists between the `Tag` and `Post` entities.

Various queries related to tags and posts are given next:

```
// Retrieving all posts for a tag, given its slug
Tag.findOne({ "slug": "nosql-engines" },
  function(err, tag) {
    Post.find({ "tag": tag }, function(err, posts) {
      posts.forEach(function(p, i) {
        console.log("%d: %s", i, p.title);
      });
    });
});
// Retrieve all associated tags for a post, given its slug
Post.findOne({ "slug": "starting-with-no-sql" })
  .populate("tags")
  .exec(function(err, post) {
    if(!err) {
      console.log("Post: " + post.title);
      post.tags.forEach(function(tag) {
        console.log(" Tag: " + tag.name);
      });
    }
});
// Inserting a post and associating tags
Tag.find({ "tags": { $in: [ "nosql", "benefits" ] } },
  function(err, tags) {
  var post = new Post({
    "title": "Benefits of NoSQL",
    "slug": "benefits-of-nosql",
    "tags": tags
  });
  post.save(function(err, post) {
    if(!err) {
      console.log("post saved successfully");
    }
  });
});
// Associating a new, non-existent, tag to a post
var tag = new Tag({
  name: "Technology",
  slug: "technology"
});
```

```
tag.save(function(err, savedTag) {
  if(!err) {
    Post.findOne({ slug: "benefits-of-nosql" })
      .populate("tags")
      .exec(function(err, post) {
        if(!err && post) {
          post.tags.push(savedTag);
          post.save(function(err, savedPost) { });
        }
      });
  }
});
// Disassociating a tag from a post
Tag.findOne({ "slug": "future-technologies" },
  function(err, tag) {
    if(!err && tag) {
      Post.findOne({ "slug": "benefits-of-nosql",
        function(err, post) {
          var idx = post.tags.indexOf(tag._id);
          post.tags.removeAt(idx);
          post.save(function(e, savedPost) { });
        });
    }
});
// Deleting a tag and updating all associated posts
Tag.findOne({ "slug": "sql-arena" },
  function(err, tag) {
    if(!err && tag) {
      var id = tag._id;
      Post.find({ "tags": tag },
        function(e, posts) {
          posts.forEach(function(p) {
            p.removeAt(p.indexOf(id));
          });
          Post.collection.insert(posts,
            function(e, savedPosts) {
          });
          tag.remove(function(e) { });
        });
    }
});
```

Miscellaneous queries

The queries that we have explored so far have tried to address the relational nature of the data and how to query a non-relational database.

Let us investigate some more queries that may be required in general for this application and what changes may be required, either in the model or otherwise, to support effective execution of these queries.

Pagination

On the landing page, we do not want to show all the posts but limit them to a maximum number. Similarly, we may want to create archive pages—annual and monthly—which requires limiting retrieval by creation date. Additionally, the posts must be sorted in reverse chronology.

In yet another scenario of pagination, we may want to show only two latest comments for a post and load all comments only on demand, say, when a user clicks on a "Show More" link or otherwise.

- **Limiting result set size**: All databases, NoSQL or otherwise, support limiting the records returned by a query. MongoDB provides the `limit` function (`http://bit.ly/ZDRYvh`) that controls the number of records returned.

- **Skipping records**: MongoDB provides the `skip` function (`http://bit.ly/ZLUEKZ`) to control from where it begins returning results. Though available, this method is best avoided. According to the official documentation:

  The cursor.skip() method is often expensive because it requires the server to walk from the beginning of the collection or index to get the offset or skip position before beginning to return results. As offset increases, cursor.skip() will become slower and more CPU intensive. With larger collections, cursor.skip() may become IO bound.

  Consider using range-based pagination for these kinds of tasks. That is, query for a range of objects, using logic within the application to determine the pagination rather than the database itself. This approach features better index utilization, if you do not need to easily jump to a specific page.

- **Sorting result set**: Not all NoSQL databases provide support for sorting the result set. For example, CouchDB always returns data sorted by key. Cassandra, on the other hand, supports sorting at configuration level, which means that you cannot sort a column that is not preconfigured for sorting `http://bit.ly/Xr3Jox`. Cassandra configuration to support sorting will be similar to the code shown as follows:

```
//Cassandra ColumnFamily configuration for sorting
<Keyspace Name="Post">
  <ColumnFamily Name="CreationTime"
              CompareWith="TimeUUIDType" />
  <ColumnFamily Name="Author "
              CompareWith="UTF8Type" />
</Keyspace>
```

As far as MongoDB is concerned, it provides the `sort` function to sort the result set. However, one must be careful not to sort a large result based on a property that is not indexed `http://docs.mongodb.org/manual/reference/method/cursor.sort/`. It would be advisable to first limit the result set and then sort the subset.

Having said that, we can get into a more complex scenario where we may want to show limited records by first sorting. The best that can be done is to ensure that the property or properties on which the sorting is required must be indexed.

Coming back to our scenario of supporting pagination while viewing the posts that must be shown in reverse chronology, the final code is as follows:

```
// Pagination: Show 5 posts per page
// Define and ensure indexes
Post.collection.ensureIndex({ lastUpdateTime: -1 });
// Show posts on the main page - latest 5 posts
Post.find()
  .sort({ lastUpdateTime: -1 })
  .limit(5)
  .exec(function(e, posts) {
    if(!e) {
      posts.forEach(function(p) {
        console.log(p.title);
      });
    }
});
// Showing 5 posts on nth page
var n = getPageNumber();
```

```
Post.find()
  .sort({ lastUpdateTime: -1 })
  .skip((n - 1) * 5)
  .limit(5)
  .exec(function(e, posts) {
    if(!e) {
      posts.forEach(function(p) {
        console.log(p.title);
      });
    }
  });
// Retrieving all comments with the associated post
var pslug = getPostSlug();

Post.findOne({ slug: pslug }, function(e, p) {
  if(!e && p) {
    Comment.find({ post: p }, function(e, comments) {
    });
  }
});
```

Limiting items in an array in result set

In our current schema, we do not really have a use case to limit the number of items in an array in result set. We will revisit this when we discuss refinements to the models.

Plugin and dynamic data support

The scariest part of designing a store for an application that supports plugin model is extensibility of the schema itself with, optional, support for query across its properties.

With a document store, this becomes simpler to do. Each plugin can define its own schema and store data in the format appropriate for consumption.

Mongoose provides a `Schema.Types.Mixed` data type `http://bit.ly/12jACJr` to support latent schema.

At a high level, plugin schema may be similar to the following:

```
// Schema for Plug-in
var entityPlugin = {
  pluginId: String, // unique id for the plugin
  owner: String,    // the plugin owner
  pluginData: Schema.Types.Mixed
};
```

```
// Making any changes to mixed value requires care
var pluginObj = new Plugin({
  pluginId: "com.m10v.blog.plugins.p1",
  owner: "Gaurav Vaish",
  pluginData: {
    "prop1": [ "value", "1" ]
  }
});
// Initial save, results in insert
pluginObj.save();
// Update the value
pluginObj.pluginData["prop2"] = { "something": "new" };
// Must mark this property as modified, save again
pluginObj.markModified("pluginData");
pluginObj.save();
```

Model refinements

As you notice in one-to-many and many-to-many relationship scenarios, we need to fire multiple queries. The primary reason is that we still have a strong normalized structure with cross-entity references using IDs.

References using non-ID property

In our application, we would typically have slug from incoming request—of the post, tag, or category. Since the slug uniquely identifies the item, we can use the slug as the record identified (value of the _id property). We, however, lose a couple of things:

- The _id property is immutable. MongoDB does not allow any change in its value. The only way out is by deleting existing records and creating a new one. Generally, slug is closely related to the title of the post or name of the category or tag. As such, we lose the ability to change them.

- By default, the autogenerated value has the timestamp of record creation in its leading 12 bits. As such, sorting by _id automatically sorts in order of the creation time—useful for sorting posts in reverse chronology. Choosing a type that is not ObjectId means we need to create another property to hold the information and ensure that it is indexed.

Because of these two key considerations, it is generally not advisable to use the custom _id property but to use default instead.

So, to get the latest posts in a category or for a tag, what can we do better?

How about storing the tag or category slug in the post record itself? Whenever we get the slug from incoming requests, we do not have to first fetch the tag or category and then get all the posts.

 Some of the scenarios mentioned in this section are inspired by the presentation *Schema Design By Example, Emily Stolfo*. Original presentation is available at http://bit.ly/YX9Bax.

The updated code with these changes reflected therein will be as follows:

```javascript
// Post - no creationTime, updated types of category, tags
var entityPost = {
  title: String,
  slug: String,
  author: String,
  lastUpdateTime: { type: Date, "default": Date.now },
  text: String,
  category: { type: String },
  tags: [ String ]
};
Post.collection.ensureIndex({ category: -1 },
  { unique: true },
  function(e) {
});
// Get all posts in a category
var slug = getCategorySlugFromRequest();
Post.find({ category: slug }, function(e, posts) {
  if(!e && posts) {
    posts.forEach(function(p) {
      console.log(p.title + " posted at "
        p._id.getTimestamp());
    });
  }
});
// Change category of a post
var catSlug = getSlugOfNewCategory();
// Note that post can be searched by using any method
//  findOne, findById or find for multiple posts
Post.findById(idOfPost, function(e, post) {
  if(!e && post) {
    post.category = catSlug;
    post.save();
  }
```

```
});
// Delete a category and move orphan posts to default
var oldCat = getSlugOfCategoryToDelete();
var newCat = getSlugOfDefaultCategory();
Post.find({ category: oldCat }, function(e, posts) {
  if(!e && posts) {
    posts.forEach(function(p) {
      p.category = newCat;
    });
    Post.collection.insert(posts, function(e) { });
    Category.findOne({ slug, oldCat },
      function(e, c) {
        c.remove();
      });
  }
});
```

Similar code will apply for working with tags.

> We are able to use slug instead of id for two reasons.
> Firstly, slug is unique. Secondly, slug is the only
> information that we get from an incoming request on
> category or tag pages. Had we a different scenario, different
> inputs available, our approach may have been different.

Denormalization and document embedding

When a user visits a post page, comments must also be shown—either latest few or all. From the incoming request, we have access to the post slug.

We need to fire two queries to retrieve this information because Post and Comment are stored in separate documents (see the following code):

```
// Retrieving all comments with the associated post
var pslug = getPostSlug();
Post.findOne({ slug: pslug }, function(e, p) {
  if(!e && p) {
    Comment.find({ post: p }, function(e, comments) {
    });
  }
});
```

Complete document embedding

We can denormalize and embed the comments along with the post so that when comments can be retrieved with the post in a single query.

To implement this, the updated schema of the Post entity will be as shown in the following code snippet:

```
// Entity Post
var entityPost = {
  title: String,
  slug: String,
  author: String,
  lastUpdateTime: { type: Date, "default": Date.now },
  text: String,
  category: String,
  tags: [ String ]
  comments: [{
    time: Date,
    author: String,
    comment: String
  }]
};
```

Notice that the comments property is no longer an array of many ObjectId, but a well-defined document structure. This approach is also referred to as **subdocument** because the item in a document with a schema of its own but part of a larger document is referred to as its **parent document**.

With this schema, the updated queries will be as follows:

```
// Retrieve a post with comments
var pslug = getSlugFromRequest();
Post.findOne({ slug: pslug }, function(e, post) {
  if(!e && post) {
    var comments = post.comments;
  }
});
// Add a comment
var newComment = getCommentJSONToAdd();
Post.findOne({ slug: pslug }, function(e, post) {
  if(!e && post) {
    post.comments.push(newComment);
    post.markModified("comments");
    post.save();
```

```
    }
  });
  // Comments Pagination: Retrieve latest 5 comments
  Post.findOne({ slug: pslug })
    .slice("comments", -5)
    .exec(function(e, post) {

  });
  // Comments Pagination: Show Nth set of comments
  Post.findOne({ slug: pslug })
    .slice("comments", [ - 5*N, 5 ])
    .exec(function(e, post) {

  });
```

Key advantages of this approach are:

- Single query for all CRUD operations related to a post and its comments
- All comments and post are co-located in the cluster—faster query
- All operations, because they are done in a single query, are atomic

Though this approach looks awesome, there is a risk of the document quickly growing large and hitting the document size limit.

Partial document embedding

One of the options to solve the previous problem is to decouple Post and Comments but keep all comments at one place. So, we come up with a different entity—Comments—and update the schema of Post to reflect the changes.

```
  // Entity Comments
  var entityComments = {
    postSlug: String,
    entries: [{
      name: String,
      time: Date,
      comment: String
    }]
  };
  var entityPost = {
    //Other properties are same, only comments changes
    comments: { type: Schema.Types.ObjectId,
              ref: "Comments" }
  };
  // Pagination: Latest 5 comments for a post
  Comments.findOne({ postSlug: pslug })
```

```
    .slice("entries", -5)
    .exec(function(e, c) {
});
// Pagination: Nth set of comments
Comments.findOne({ postSlug: pslug })
    .slice("entries", [ -5*N, 5 ])
    .exec(function(e, c) {
});
// Inserting a new comment
var commentObj = getJSONForNewComment();
Comments.findOne({ postSlug: pslug },
    function(e, c) {
        c.entries.push(commentObj);
});
```

This approach ensures fixed Post document size (barring the actual content size restriction) as well as atomic commits to the related Comments record.

There are a few disadvantages to this approach:

- Comments records still can hit the document size limit.
- Comments can be stored in a separate physical location in the cluster as compared to the associated Post. Query, as such, can be slower.

Bucketing

In both the approaches of document embedding discussed earlier, we run into the risk of hitting document size limit. Using the earlier denormalized form means slower retrievals because records can be anywhere in the cluster and non-atomic commits because all records are independent.

How about using a mix of the two? What I mean is, store multiple comments in one record but limit the number of comments—we store no more than a fixed number of comments per record—say, 10.

Make one change to the Comments schema, add a commentCount property that keeps a track of number of actual comments in the record:

```
// Entity Post
var entityComments = {
    postSlug: String,
    commentCount: int,
    entries: [{
        name: String,
        time: Date,
        comment: String
```

```
    }]
  };
  // Inserting a new comment - use upsert
  var commentObj = getJSONForNewComment();
  Comments.update({
    postSlug: slug,
    commentCount: { $lt: 10 }, {
      $inc: { commentCount: 1 },
      $push: { entries: commentObj },
    }, {
      upsert: true
    }
    function(e, c) {
  });
```

Note that we not only have been able to limit the document size but also achieve atomicity while adding a new comment that can result in either updating an existing record or creating a new record.

We still have storage fragmentation but a controlled one this time.

As another optimization, you may want to update the Post record with the reference of the Comments record updated or created. This will help retrieving the latest comments given in a post without searching across the comments collection.

Cache document approach

A feature that I would want on my blog is latest comments across posts. It will give the viewers a picture about what is being currently discussed on my blog. Similarly, I may want to show latest comments by a specific user.

If we use completely normalized form where each comment is stored separately, this is a trivial problem to solve. However, because using one comment per record can result in slow retrieval, we want to solve this problem by using the embedded document approach.

```
// Latest comments in normalized form

Comment.find()
  .sortBy( { _id: -1 })
  .limit(10).exec(function(e, comments) {
});

// Latest comments by a user
```

```
Comment.find({ author: name })
  .sortBy( { _id: -1 })
  .imit(10).exec(function(e, comments) {
});
```

One of the options to solve this problem is to keep the latest comments in cache that can be updated; better to persist with this so that they doesn"t get evicted if not used for long.

We can have records to keep these frequently queried and less-frequently updated data. Specifically for comments, there can be one document that keeps a list of the latest comments added. If we need to show 10 latest comments, it may have more than 10, even 100 comments. A representative structure may be:

```
// Cache document definition
var entityCacheDoc = {
  _id: String,
updateTime: Date,
  validity: Date,
  value: [ { } ]
};
// Retrieving latest 5 comments from cache document
CacheDoc.findById("comments")
  .slice("value", -5)
  .exec(function(e, doc) {
});
```

The following steps are required to maintain this structure:

- When adding a comment, add it to Comments as well as the CacheDoc collection
- When retrieving the latest comments to show, use the CacheDoc collection
- Run a job at optimal frequency, based on the frequency at which new comments are created, that will cleanup the comments in CacheDoc

Miscellaneous changes

The last scenario that we will look into is retrieving comments by a specific user.

In embedded document mode, searching for comments by a specific user can be a very costly affair. The code to search for all comments is:

```
//Search for comments by a user
Post.find({ "comments.author": name })
  .select({ comments: 1 })
  .exec(function(e, posts) {
});
```

This works perfectly fine. The only problem is performance. If, on an average, there are 100 comments per post and an author commented on 5 posts, 500 comments will be scanned. One way to solve this problem is create another set of documents that will have reference to comments made by a user per post—that"s redundancy, commonly used with NoSQL.

In case of normalized comments where we have one comment per record, scanning for comments by a user is extremely efficient. Note that this has severe performance drawbacks as noticed earlier.

As with any storage system, it is impossible to optimize all the parameters. You can trade-off one against the other.

Summary

In this chapter we took a pragmatic view of working with NoSQL. The scenarios covered —single entity query, aggregates, one-to-one, one-to-many, and many-to-many relationships—should give you a strong head start implementing NoSQL for your application.

We learnt two key aspects of modeling for NoSQL—denormalization of data and modeling for queries. Denormalization ensures that cross-entity accesses (aka JOIN) are reduced while query-driven modeling ensures that you do not invent new fancy techniques while writing queries rather than use the models directly. The latter approach not only ensures simplified and maintainable queries but also faster execution.

We explored various approaches of modeling in document store and went deep into pros and cons of each approach, what they offer and where they negatively impact the application.

More often than not, the applications where NoSQL is desirable have a lot more reads than writes. Apart from caching the responses at the HTTP layer, using cache documents is also a useful approach where the caches can not only be persisted but also queried and partially updated.

You may have to use one approach for one entity and another for a different entity. Pick the ones that suit you best in your specific case. Just to reiterate, the answer may work in SQL as well.

A
Taxonomy

The taxonomy introduces you to common and not-so-common terms that we come across while dealing with NoSQL. This also enables you to read through and understand the literature available on the Internet or otherwise.

Vocabulary

In this section, we will glance through the vocabulary that you need to understand; and take a deep dive into NoSQL databases later in the book.

Data store: A store that keeps the data persisted so that it can be retrieved even after application ends or computer restarts.

Database: A data store that keeps and allows access to the data in a structured manner.

Database Management System (DBMS): A software application that controls working (creation, access, maintenance, and general purpose use) with a database.

Relational DBMS (RDBMS): A software application that not only stores the data but also the relation between them. RDBMS is based on the relational model developed by Edgar Frank Codd in 1970. RDBMS uses the notion of tables, columns, and rows to manipulate the data, and of foreign keys to specify the relationships.

Structured Query Language (SQL): A special-purpose programming language to interact with RDBMS.

Foreign key constraint: This is a referential constraint between two tables. It is a column or a set of columns in one table referred to as the child table that refers to a column or a set of columns in another table referred to as the parent table. The values in a row of the child table must be one of the values in the rows of the parent table for the corresponding column or columns.

NoSQL: A class of DBMS that does not use SQL. Specifically, the NoSQL databases do not store any relationships across the data in itself. They must be manipulated at the application level., if at all.

Normalization: The process of organizing the records (tables and columns) to minimize the redundancy. The process typically involves splitting the data across multiple tables and defining relationships between them. Edgar F. Codd, the inventor of the relational model, introduced this concept in 1970.

Normal Form: The structure of database left after the process of normalization is referred to as Normal Form. Codd introduced the first Normal Form (1NF) in 1970. Subsequently, he defined the second and the third Normal Forms (2NF and 3NF) in 1971. Together with Raymond F. Boyce, he created Boyce-Codd Normal Form (BCNF or 3.5NF) in 1974. Each Normal Form is progressively built upon the previous one and adds stronger rules to remove redundancy.

Denormalization: The inverse of normalization, this process increases the speed of data access by grouping related data, introducing duplicity and redundancy.

Primary key: A key to uniquely identify a record or row in a table in database—relational or otherwise. Primary keys are indexed by a DBMS to allow faster access.

Transaction: Group of operations in database that must all succeed or cause the entire group to rollback for database to operate meaningfully.

CRUD: Four key operations with the records of a database—create, retrieve, update, and delete.

Atomicity, Consistency, Isolation, Durability (ACID): ACID is the set of properties that database transactions should have.

JavaScript Object Notation (JSON): JSON is a compact format to represent objects. It was originally specified by Douglas Crockford and outlined in RFC 4627. Though a subset of the JavaScript language specification, JSON is a language-independent format and the parsers and serializers are available in most of the languages today. Most of the NoSQL databases support JSON for entity representation.

Multi-Version Concurrency Control (MVCC): It is a mechanism to provide concurrent access. For ACID compliance, MVCC helps implement isolation. It is used by RDBMS database PostgreSQL as well as NoSQL databases like CouchDB and MongoDB.

Basic availability: Each query or request must be responded to with either a success or failed result. More the successful results, the better the system.

Soft state: The state of the system may change over time, at times without input. The few the changes without input, the better the system.

Eventual consistency: The system may be momentarily inconsistent but will be consistent eventually. The duration of eventuality is left to the system. It may range from microseconds to tens of milliseconds to even seconds. The shorter the duration, the better the system.

BASE: The set of properties—basic availability, soft state, and eventual consistency—that a distributed database can inhibit.

CAP theorem: Also known as the Brewer's theorem, states that it is impossible for a distributed computer system to simultaneously provide consistency, availability, and partition tolerance, maximum two of the three can be provided at any given point in time.

Relationship between CAP, ACID, and NoSQL

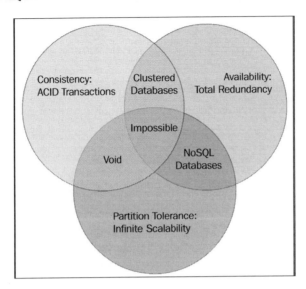

Though there is no rule that NoSQL databases cannot provide ACID transactions, their very purpose is defeated. That's why you see them providing availability and horizontal scaling.

Having said that, CouchDB and Neo4j are two examples of NoSQL databases that provide strong consistency and are ACID compliant.

Because of the need for speed with eventual (not immediate) consistency, denormalization may be brought in to increase redundancy at the cost of space and immediate consistency.

Index

IDL 84
Interface Definition Language. *See* IDL

J

JavaScript Object Notation. *See* JSON
JSON 117

K

Key-value store
  about 41
  advantages 42
  Berkley DB 41
  example 42, 43
  Memcached 41
  MemcacheDB 41
  Redis 41
  Voldemort 41

L

Lucene 9

M

map and reduce functions 35
MapReduce 8
MAU 86
MCC 21
me attribute 32
MemcacheDB 59
miscellaneous queries
  about 103
  arrays, limiting 105
  dynamic data support 105
  pagination 103, 104
  plugin 105
model refinements
  about 106
  cache document approach 112, 113
  denormalization 108-111
  document embedding 108-111
  miscellaneous changes 113, 114
  references, non-ID property used 106-108

models
  comparing 47, 48
MongoDB
  about 37, 59, 91
  setup 91
  used, for store application implementation
    90, 91
Monthly Active Users. *See* MAU
multi-storage type databases
  Aerospike 46
  ArangoDB 46
  OrientDB 46
multitenancy 78
Multiversion concurrency control. *See* MCC
Multi-Version Concurrency Control. *See*
    MVCC
MVCC 117

N

Neo4j 59
nontechnical comparison
  community 86
  license 85
  source 85
  vendor support 86
normal form 116
normalization 116
NoSQL
  advantages 51
  application, categories 51
  characteristics 13
  computing ecosystem 8
  databases 11
  defining 8
  drawbacks 51
  history 8
  need for 11
  overview 7
  storage types 25
NoSQL approach
  about 20
  complex queries 20
  data update 21
  scalability 21
  schema flexibility 20

Thank you for buying
Getting Started with NoSQL

About Packt Publishing

Packt, pronounced 'packed', published its first book "*Mastering phpMyAdmin for Effective MySQL Management*" in April 2004 and subsequently continued to specialize in publishing highly focused books on specific technologies and solutions.

Our books and publications share the experiences of your fellow IT professionals in adapting and customizing today's systems, applications, and frameworks. Our solution based books give you the knowledge and power to customize the software and technologies you're using to get the job done. Packt books are more specific and less general than the IT books you have seen in the past. Our unique business model allows us to bring you more focused information, giving you more of what you need to know, and less of what you don't.

Packt is a modern, yet unique publishing company, which focuses on producing quality, cutting-edge books for communities of developers, administrators, and newbies alike. For more information, please visit our website: www.packtpub.com.

Writing for Packt

We welcome all inquiries from people who are interested in authoring. Book proposals should be sent to author@packtpub.com. If your book idea is still at an early stage and you would like to discuss it first before writing a formal book proposal, contact us; one of our commissioning editors will get in touch with you.

We're not just looking for published authors; if you have strong technical skills but no writing experience, our experienced editors can help you develop a writing career, or simply get some additional reward for your expertise.

CouchDB and PHP Web Development Beginner's Guide

ISBN: 978-1-849513-58-6   Paperback: 304 pages

Get your PHP application from conception to deployment by leveraging CouchDB's robust features

1. Build and deploy a flexible Social Networking application using PHP and leveraging key features of CouchDB to do the heavy lifting

2. Explore the features and functionality of CouchDB, by taking a deep look into Documents, Views, Replication, and much more.

3. Conceptualize a lightweight PHP framework from scratch and write code that can easily port to other frameworks

HBase Administration Cookbook

ISBN: 978-1-849517-14-0   Paperback: 332 pages

Master HBase configuration and administration for optimum database performance

1. Complete guide to building Facebook applications in PHP

2. Fully illustrated with fun, functional step-by-step examples

3. Covers recent platform additions: Facebook JavaScript, Facebook AJAX

4. Create data-driven applications, employ multimedia, and more

Please check **www.PacktPub.com** for information on our titles

Printed in Great Britain
by Amazon.co.uk, Ltd.,
Marston Gate.